FIELD GUIDE TO

Beaufortias, Eremaeas, Kunzeas & Regelias

Kunzea spathulata

First published in 2019
by Rob Sainsbury's Wildflower Books (ABN: 13 892 524 568)
Bull Creek Western Australia 6149

This book is copyright. Apart from any fair dealing, for the purposes of study, research, criticism, review or as otherwise permitted under the Copyright Act, no part may be reproduced by any process without written permission. Enquiries should be made to the publisher.
Copyright Robert Malcolm Sainsbury 2019.

National Library of Australia
Cataloguing-in-Publication data

Sainsbury, R.M. (Robert Malcolm), 1950-
Field Guide to Beaufortias, Eremaeas, Kunzeas and Regelias

Includes index

ISBN 978-0-6485125-2-3

1. Myrtaceae – Identification. 2 Wildflowers – Western Australia. 1. Title.

Printed by: Snap Print, Applecross, Western Australia.

Cover photo: Kunzea jucunda

Synopsis

This book is designed to function as a Wildflower Field Guide to assist in the field identification of a selection of predominantly Western Australian plants in the Myrtle family (Myrtaceae).
I have focused on all the named West Australian species of Beaufortia, Kunzea, Eremaea & Regelia - names perhaps unfamiliar to enthusiasts but very prominent in the south west of WA during our Widflower season.
The Kunzeas are the only genus found elsewhere in Australia. I have included a small selection of eastern Australian ones in this work to perhaps widen the interest.
The majority of images are mine but there are a few for which I have not been able to obtain photographs – Eastern Australian species and flowering species I was unsuccessful in locating during my field trips. Those particular photos are listed in the Acknowledgements section of this manuscript.

Personally, I prefer to photograph plants in their natural environment, and not in a studio situation.

I have endeavored to confirm the identity of all plant species featured in the manuscript at the Western Australian Herbarium.
The work, however, is not intended to be the definitive work on these genera.
It should be noted that botanical research generally, and botanical nomenclature (taxonomy)
in particular, is a continually ongoing process?
At present, there is some considerable discussion among taxonomists that a number of plants from the West Australian Myrtle family – including the genera Beaufortia, Eremaea & Regelia – should be included in the genus Melaleuca.
However, this hasn't yet been confirmed, and I felt that these plants were well worth featuring in a dedicated 'Field Guide'; of interest to wildflower enthusiasts throughout Australia and perhaps worldwide. I would also hope the work would be a useful source of reference material for horticultural students and Botanists.

INTRODUCTION
Beaufortia ("Bottlebrushes")

Beaufortia is a genus of woody shrubs and small trees in the family Myrtaceae, only found in the South West of Western Australia. The genus *Beaufortia* is closely related to the Genera *Melaleuca*, *Calothamnus*, *Regelia* and others. The difference has been considered as mainly in the way the anthers are attached to the stalks of the stamens, and in the way they open to release their pollen. *Beaufortia* anthers are attached at one end and open by splitting into 2 slits at the other.

Description

Plants in the genus *Beaufortia*, sometimes commonly known as bottlebrush, are evergreen shrubs with very small, glandular, aromatic leaves usually oppositely arranged and can grow up to 3m in height. Flowers appear in spikes or heads. Many have a mixture of male and bisexual flowers on one plant. The flower has triangular sepals which can be glabrous or ciliate; the petals are generally small and ciliate, the stamens are often in bundles of five and vary in colour from red, purple, orange, pink and occasionally white. The petals usually fall off as the flower opens, or shortly after that. Flowering in most species occurs between spring and autumn. A few species can flower all year round. The fruit is a woody capsule.

Taxonomy and naming

The first formal description of the genus *Beaufortia* was published in 1812 by Robert Brown in William Aiton's Hortus Kewensis. It was followed by a description of the first-named species, *Beaufortia decussata*. The genus was named after the Duchess of Beaufort Mary Somerset.

In *Curtis's Botanical Magazine* it is noted that 'her grace possessed a flourishing botanical garden at her seat, at Badminton, in Gloucestershire'.

Some taxonomists have suggested that *Beaufortia* along with other genera including *Calothamnus*, *Conothamnus*, *Eremaea*, *Phymatocarpus* and *Regelia* should be included in the genus *Melaleuca* but the change has not yet been adopted by most herbaria.

Distribution and habitat

All species of *Beaufortia* occur in the South West of Western Australia, found as far north as Shark Bay and as far south as Esperance. Beaufortias are often found in sand plain and in heath, although *Beaufortia sparsa* will grow in marshy places and is subsequently known by the common name Swamp Bottlebrush.

Conservation

Some species of *Beaufortia* are common within their range but Beaufortia bicolor, B. burbidgeae, B. eriocephala and B. purpurea are classified as 'Priority Three' by the Western Australian Government Department of Parks and Wildlife, meaning that they are known from only a few locations but not necessarily under imminent threat.

B. raggedensis, however, is classified as 'Priority Two', by the West Australian DPW, meaning that it is more at risk. It has a highly restricted distribution, within a National Park.

Use in cultivation

All the species of *Beaufortia* are worth growing in the garden but few have been grown successfully - particularly in Eastern Australia. They generally require full sun and excellent drainage.

Eremaea

Eremaea is a genus of woody shrubs and small trees in the family Myrtaceae and is endemic to the south-west of Western Australia. Little study of the genus as a whole had been undertaken until Roger Hnatiuk researched *Eremaea* and published a paper in 1993, *A revision of the genus Eremaea (Myrtaceae)* in Nuytsia. The first species to be described was *Eremaea pauciflora* (as *Metrosideros pauciflora*) in 1837 and by 1964, the number of species known had increased to 12. Hnatiuk recognised 16 species, 5 subspecies and a number of varieties.

Description

Plants in the genus *Eremaea* are shrubs or small trees with small leaves that are arranged alternately on the stem and are dotted with oil glands. The flowers have both male and female parts and are solitary or in clusters of two or three on the ends of the branches. There are 5 sepals, and 5 petals which fall off as the flower matures. There are many stamens, all longer than the petals and usually arranged in groups of five. The stamens give the flowers their colour, which may be pink, deep pink, orange or violet. The fruit is a woody capsule containing one to six small seeds.

Taxonomy and naming

The genus *Eremaea* was first named and formally described in 1839 by John Lindley in 'A Sketch of the Vegetation of the Swan River Colony' in which he noted "Of this genus, which may be called *Eremaea* ... there are three species, of which the only pretty kind is *E. fimbriata*." (The species now known as *Eremaea pauciflora* had been described earlier but given the name *Metrosideros pauciflora*.)

The genus *Eremaea* is closely related to *Melaleuca, Beaufortia Regelia* and several others, differing mainly in the way the anthers are attached to the stalks of the stamens, and in the way they open to release their pollen. *Eremaea* is most closely related to *Regelia* and *Calothamnus* as these groups have anthers that open by longitudinal slits or pores. *Eremaea* can be distinguished from *Regelia* by the number of flowers in the flowering heads - in *Regelia* the flowers are in dense heads, whereas in *Eremaea* they are solitary or in groups of two or three. *Calothamnus* species have longer leaves than both of these genera. In 2014, Lyndley Craven and others proposed, mainly on the basis of DNA evidence, that species in the genus *Eremaea*, along with those in *Callistemon, Conothamnus, Calothamnus, Phymatocarpus* and *Regelia* be transferred to *Melaleuca*.

However, this change has not yet been adopted by most herbaria.

The name *Eremaea* is from a poetic Greek word *eremaios* meaning "solitary", referring to the few-flowered inflorescences on the ends of the branches.

Distribution and habitat

Eremaea are found only in the south-west of Western Australia.

Conservation

Most species of *Eremaea* are common within their range.

However, *Eremaea blackwelliana*, is listed as "Priority four" by the Western Australian Government Department of Parks and Wildlife meaning that it is considered 'rare and endangered'.

Eremaea acutifolia is classified as "Priority Three" by the Western Australian Government Wildlife. It is known from only a few locations, although not yet under imminent threat.

Use in cultivation

Some species of *Eremaea* have been grown in cultivation; but with varying success. *Eremaea beaufortioides* has grown well in sunny situations with excellent drainage producing a vigorous, spreading shrub. Grafting onto *Kunzea ambigua* has been successful. Some other species grow well in Kings Park but are rarely seen in the eastern states. Their orange colour, not common in Australian natives, and their habit of having flowers on the ends of their branches make them worthy garden subjects

Kunzea

Kunzea is a genus of plants in the family Myrtaceae and is endemic to Australasia. They are shrubs, sometimes small trees and usually have small, crowded, rather aromatic leaves. The flowers are similar to those of plants in the genus *Leptospermum* but differ in having stamens that are longer than the petals. Most Kunzeas are endemic to Western Australia but about a third of them occur in eastern Australia and a few are found in New Zealand.

Description

Plants in the genus *Kunzea* are shrubs or small trees, usually with their leaves arranged alternately along the branches. The flowers are arranged in clusters near the ends of the branches, which in some species, continue to grow after flowering. The flowers of most species lack a stalk but those that have one are usually solitary or in groups of two or three. In some species, the flowers are surrounded by enlarged bracts. There are five petals, five sepals and a large number of stamens which are always longer than the petals. The fruit is a usually a woody capsule. Kunzeas are similar to species in other genera of the Myrtaceae, especially *Leptospermum* but are distinguished from that genus by having stamens that are longer than the petals.

Taxonomy and naming

The first formal description of a kunzea was published in 1828 by Ludwig Reichenbach in his book *Conspectus Regni Vegetabilis*. Reichenbach referred to three species - *K. capitata*, *K. ericifolia* and *K. corifolia* (now *K. ambigua* but did not nominate a type species. In 1981, Hellmut Toelken nominated K. *capitata* as the type species. Reichenbach named the genus after his "distinguished friend", the German naturalist Gustave Kunze, professor of botany in Leipzig. The taxonomy of the genus is not settled and hybrids often occur where two species occur in the same area.

Distribution

The majority of *Kunzea* species are endemic to the south-west of Western Australia but there are species in every Australian state and in New Zealand.

Conservation

Some species of *Kunzea* are common within their range but K. eriocalyx is classified as "Priority two" by the Western Australian Government Department of Parks and Wildlife, meaning that it is known from only one or a few locations. that are potentially at risk.

K. pauciflora was classified as "Priority four" by the W.A.G.D.P.W. in 1995/1996, meaning, that at the time, it was facing extinction, or at least, considered by W.A.G.D.P.W. as rare and endangered. K. newbeyi is classified as "Priority one" by W.A.G.D.P.W. It is known from only one location that is potentially at risk.

Use in horticulture

Some species of *Kunzea* are suitable for use in gardens. *Kunzea ambigua* is described as a "handsome shrub which attracts numerous birds and colourful soldier beetles when in flower". A form of this species from southern Victoria reputedly flowers profusely with sprays of scented flowers. *Kunzea capitata* and *K. pulchella* are red-flowering species and are described as "indeed outstanding" although they are sometimes difficult to establish in eastern Australia and need to be grafted onto hardier rootstock.

Regelia

Regelia is a genus of flowering plants in the family Myrtaceae and is endemic to the south-west of Western Australia. The genus is composed of five species of small leaved, evergreen shrubs which have heads of flowers on the ends of branches which continue to grow after flowering.

Description

Plants in the genus *Regelia* are woody, evergreen shrubs ranging in height from 1–6 meters. Their leaves are small, arranged in opposite pairs or spirally and are noted for bearing essential oils. The flowers are pinkish purple, sometimes red, and are arranged in heads on the ends of branches which continue to grow after flowering. The flowers have 5 sepals, 5 petals and numerous stamens arranged in 5 bundles around the edge of the flower. They differ to other genera in the Myrtaceae Family in the attachment of the anthers to their stalks; the way they open to release their pollen, and the number of seeds in the fruits. Plants in the genus have their anthers attached at the base (rather than the side) and open at terminal pores (rather than slits). The fruits are woody capsules, generally with three valves, and have a maximum of two fertile seeds in each valve.

Taxonomy and naming

The genus *Regelia* was first formally described in 1843 by J.C.Schauer in the journal *Linnaea; Ein Journal für die Botanik in ihrem ganzen Umfange* and the first species he named was *Regelia ciliata*. The name '*Regelia*' honors the German gardener and botanist Eduard August von Regel.

Distribution and habitat

All five *Regelia* species are found in. the south-west of Western Australia only. They grow in sandy soil, often on the margins of winter-wet depressions.

Conservation

Two species, *Regelia cymbifolia* and *Regelia megacephala*, are classified as "Priority Four" by the Western Australian government Department of Parks and Wildlife] meaning that they are rare and endangered

CONTENTS

Beaufortia

Beaufortia aestiva -K.J. Brooks (Kalbarri Beaufortia)	20
Beaufortia anisandra –Schauer (Dark Beaufortia)	22
Beaufortia bicolor -Strid. (Badgingarra Beaufortia)	24
Beaufortia bracteosa –Diels	26
Beaufortia burbidgeae A.A.Burb. Column Beaufortia	28
Beaufortia cyrtodonta (Turcz.) Benth. (Stirling Range Bottlebrush)	30
Beaufortia decussata -R.Br. (Gravel Bottlebrush)	32
Beaufortia elegans –Schauer (Elegant Beaufortia)	34
Beaufortia empetrifolia (Rchb.) Schauer (South Coast Beaufortia)	36
Beaufortia eriocephala -W.Fitz. (Woolly Bottlebrush)	38
Beaufortia incana (Benth.) A.S. George (Grey-leaved Beaufortia)	40
Beaufortia kwonganicola -A.A. Burb. (Lesueur Beaufortia)	42
Beaufortia macrostemon -Lindl. (Darling Range Beaufortia)	44
Beaufortia micrantha –Schauer (Little Bottlebrush)	46
Beaufortia orbifolia -F.Muell. (Ravensthorpe Bottlebrush)	48
Beaufortia puberula -Turcz. (Hairy-leaved Beaufortia)	50
Beaufortia purpurea -Lindl. (Purple Beaufortia)	52
Beaufortia raggedensis A.A.Burb. Mount Ragged Beaufortia	54
Beaufortia schaueri –Schauer (Pink Beaufortia)	56
Beaufortia sparsa -R.Br. (Swamp Bottlebrush)	58
Beaufortia sprengelioides (DC.) Craven - Shark Bay Beaufortia	60
Beaufortia squarrosa –Schauer (Sand Beaufortia)	62

Eremaea

Eremaea acutifolia -F.Muell (Rusty Eremaea)	66
Eremaea asterocarpa Hnatiuk	68
Eremaea poss.atala Hnatiuk	70
Eremaea beaufortioides -Benth.	72

Eremaea blackwelliana Hnatiuk	74
Eremaea brevifolia (Benth.) Domin	76
Eremaea ×codonocarpa Hnatiuk	78
Eremaea dendroidea Hnatiuk	80
Eremaea ebracteata F.Muell	82
Eremaea poss.ectadioclada –Hnatiuk	84
Eremaea fimbriata Lindl.	86
Eremaea hadra Hnatiuk	88
Eremaea pauciflora (Endl.) Druce	90
Eremaea ×phoenicea Hnatiuk	92
Eremaea purpurea -C.A. Gardner	96
Eremaea violacea -F.Muell. (Violet Eremaea)	98

Kunzea

Kunzea acicularis Toelken & G.F.Craig	104
Kunzea acuminata Toelken	106
Kunzea affinis S.Moore	108
Kunzea ambigua (Sm.) Druce	110
Kunzea baxteri (Klotzsch) Schauer (Baxter's Kunzea)	112
Kunzea cambagei Maiden & Betche	114
Kunzea poss. capitata	116
Kunzea ciliata –Toelken	118
Kunzea cincinnata Toelken	120
Kunzea clavata Toelken	122
Kunzea ericifolia (Sm.) Heynh. (Spearwood)	124
Kunzea eriocalyx -F.Muell.	126
Kunzea glabrescens –Toelken	128
Kunzea jucunda Diels & E.Pritz.	130
Kunzea micrantha –Schauer	132
Kunzea micromera –Schauer	134
Kunzea montana (Diels) Domin [Mountain Kunzea]	136
Kunzea muelleri Benth.	138
Kunzea newbeyi Toelken	140
Kunzea obovata Byrnes	142
Kunzea opposita –F.Muell	144
Kunzea parvifolia –Schauer	146
Kunzea pauciflora –Schauer	148
Kunzea pomifera -F. Muell. (Muntries)	150

Kunzea praestans –Schauer 152
Kunzea preissiana –Schauer 154
Kunzea pulchella (Lindl.) A.S. George (Granite Kunzea) 156
Kunzea recurva –Schauer 158
Kunzea ×rosea (Turcz.) Govaerts 162
Kunzea rostrata Toelken 164
Kunzea salina (Trudgen & Keighery) de Lange & Toelken 166
Kunzea similis Toelken 168
Kunzea spathulata –Toelken 170
Kunzea strigosa Toelken & G.F.Craig 172
Kunzea sulphurea Tovey & P.Morris 174

Regelia

Regelia ciliata Schauer 178
Regelia cymbifolia (Diels) C.A. Gardner 180
Regelia inops (Schauer) Schauer 182
Regelia megacephala C.A Gardner 184
Regelia velutina (Turcz) 186

Acknowledgements
Barbara Rye for reviewing the manuscript.
Karen McDermott – Serenity Press: Facillitating the printing of the manuscript.
Neville Marchant for his encouragement and support.
Printer Computer Service Centre: IT Assistance.
The Western Australian Herbarium for allowing me access to their records.
Flora Base – the Western Australian Flora.

Images:
Mary Hoggart – images of Beaufortia raggedensis and Kunzea salina.

Website: *earth.com* for image of Kunzea acuminata.

Wikimedia commons – images of Kunzea ambigua, K.cambagei, K.muelleri, K.obovata K.parvifolia & K.opposita.

J Cochrane and G Cockerton – images of Kunzea similis
D Brassington, R Jasper and S Kern – images of Kunzea similis subsp. mediterranea.

References

Association of Societies for Growing Australian Plants ASGAP - Kunzea ericifolia".
2007.

Blackall, W.E. and Grieve, B.J. (1980)
How to Know Western Australian Wildflowers, Part 3A; Restructured and Revised
2nd edition by B.J. Grieve
University of Western Australian Press

Burbidge, Andrew A.
A taxonomic revision of Beaufortia (Myrtaceae: Melaleuceae)
Nuytsia (27: 165–202).

Corrick, Margaret G.; Fuhrer, Bruce A. (2009). *Wildflowers of southern Western Australia* (3rd ed.). Kenthurst, N.S.W.: Rosenberg Publishing.

Department of Parks and Wildlife, Western Australia
June 2014
Interim Recovery Plan No. 347
(*Kunzea acicularis*)
Interim Recovery Plan
2014–2019

Fairley A, Moore P (2000). Native Plants of the Sydney District: An Identification Guide (2nd ed.). Kenthurst, NSW: Kangaroo Press.

Grieg, Denise
Field Guide to Australian Wildflowers
Published in Australia by
New Holland Publishers (Australia) Pty Ltd
First published 1999. Reprinted 2014.

Hnatiuk, Roger J. (1993)
A revision of the genus *Eremaea* (Myrtaceae)
Nuytsia 9: 137-122

Holliday, Ivan
Melaleucas A Field and Garden Guide 2nd Edition
Published in Australia by Reed New Holland
an imprint of New Holland Publishers (Australia) Pty Ltd
First published 1989 Hamlyn Australia
Revised Edition published 2004 Reed New Holland.

Reprinted 2008

McAloon, Cameron. "Rare flowering plant Kunzea newbeyi found in WA's South West set to bloom". Australian Broadcasting Corporation

Marshall, Brian; Tullis, Brian (photography); Wilson, Margaret (illustrations) (1990). Wildflowers of the West Coast Hills Region : the plants and flowers of the Darling Scarp and Range in the Kalamunda Shire, the backdrop to Perth, Western Australia (revised 2002 ed.). Western Australia: Quality Publishing Australia.

Paczkowska, Grazyna; Chapman, Alex R. (2000). The Western Australian flora : a descriptive catalogue. Perth: Wildflower Society of Western Australia.

Toelken, H.R.
A revision of the genus kunzea (myrtaceae)
I. the western australian section zea1vuk
State Herbarium of South Australia, Botanic Gardens of Adelaide
North Terrace, Adelaide, South Australia 5000

Toelken, H.R.
Revision of Kunzea (Myrtaceae). 2.
Subgenera Angasomyrtus and Salisia (section Salisia) from Western Australia and subgenera Kunzea and Niviferae sections Platyphyllae and Pallidiflorae) from eastern Australia
State Herbarium of South Australia, G.P.O. Box 1047, Adelaide, South Australia 5001

Toelken, H.R. & Craig, G.F. (2007)
Kunzea acicularis, K. strigosa
and K. similis subsp.
mediterranea (Myrtaceae)
– new taxa from near Ravensthorpe, Western
Australia
Nuytsia 17: 385–396

Western Australian Herbarium (1998 –   ) Flora Base – the Western Australian Flora
Department of Biodiversity, Conservation and Attractions

Wikipedia® - registered trademark of the Wikimedia Foundation, Inc.

Wrigley, John W.; Fagg, Murray (1983). Australian native plants: a manual for their propagation, cultivation and use in landscaping (2nd ed.). Sydney: Collins.

Glossary

Appressed	pressed closely to another organ but not united.
Bracteoles	a small bract-like structure borne singly or in a pair on the pedicel or calyx of a flower.
Calyx lobe when the lower	one of the free upper parts of the calyx which may be present part is united into a tube.
Decurrant	extending downwards beyond the point of insertion.
Decussate	alternate pairs.
Depressed	flattened as if pressed down from the top or end.
Elliptic	widest at the middle, and more or less rounded at the ends.
Genus (Genera)	a genus is a taxonomic rank used in the biological classification of living and fossil organisms as well as viruses. The composition of a genus is determined by a taxonomist. The standards for genus classification are not strictly codified, so different authorities often produce different classifications for genera.
Glabrous	having a surface without hairs.
Hypanthium	a cup-shaped or tubular body formed by the conjoined sepals, petals and stamens.
Inflorescence	an inflorescence is a group or cluster of flowers arranged on a stem that is composed of a main branch or an arrangement of branches.
Kwongan	heath and low shrub land.
Lamina	the usually flattened blade of a leaf or frond.
Lanceolate	lance-shaped, long; widening above the base and tapering to a point.
Lateral	attached to the side of an organ: eg. leaves of a stem.
Laterite	a soil and rock type, rich in iron and aluminium, commonly thought to have formed in hot and tropical areas. to have formed in hot and tropical areas.
Linear	long and narrow with parallel sides (leaf).

Nuytsia	the Journal of the West Australian Herbarium.
Oblanceolate	having a lanceolate shape but broadest in the upper third.
Obovate	a 2-dimensional shape: similar to ovate.
Petal	in a flower; one of the segments or divisions of the inner whorl of non-fertile parts surrounding the fertile organs; usually soft and conspicuously coloured.
Petiole	the stalk of a leaf.
Rostrate	beaked; the apex narrowed into a slender, usually obtuse point.
Sepal	in a flower; one of the segments or divisions of the outer whorl of non-fertile parts surrounding the fertile organs; usually green.
Sessile	of a structure, when borne without a supporting part.
Specific epithet	follows the name of the Genus, and is the second word of a botanical binomial. The generic name and the specific epithet together constitute the name of a species.
,Stamen	male organ of a flower, usually consisting of a stalk (filament) and a pollen-bearing portion (anther).
Taxonomy	plant taxonomy is the science that finds, identifies, describes, classifies and names plants.
Urceolate	Shaped like an urn or pitcher, with a swollen middle and narrowing top.

18

Beaufortia
Beaufortia micrantha

Beaufortia aestiva K.J.Brooks
Kalbarri Beaufortia

Description

Beaufortia aestiva has a variable habit, occasionally growing to a height of about 4m but more usually about 2m high and 2m wide.

The leaves are egg-shaped with the narrower end towards the base, up to about 11mm long and are arranged in alternating pairs (decussate).

The flowers vary in colour, from creamy orange to red and are arranged in heads 35–45mm in diameter, on the ends of branches which continue to grow after flowering.

Flowering period is quite long. It has been recorded as early as June and as late as March, but primarily flowers from October to February. It is followed by fruit which are woody capsules up to about 9 mm long. It can be distinguished from other Beaufortias by its stamens which are in bundles of 5 to 7; 28–40mm long, joined for about half their length. This species is often confused with B.squarrosa.

There is a yellow form which is illustrated.

Taxonomy and naming

Beaufortia aestiva was first formally described in 1998 by Kristine J. Brooks in Nuytsia from a specimen found near Binnu. The specific epithet ("aestiva") is a Latin word meaning "summer"

Distribution and habitat

Beaufortia aestiva occurs North, between Kalbarri and Eneabba and in the Southeast, near Tammin and Wongan Hills. It grows on sandplains in heath and low shrubland.

Beaufortia anisandra Schauer
Dark Beaufortia

Description

Beaufortia anisandra is a densely branched shrub which grows to a height of 1.5m. The leaves are arranged in opposite pairs and are egg-shaped to lance-shaped, 3–6.5 mm long, rigid, concave in cross section with a mid vein and several faint lateral veins.

The flowers are red to dark purplish red and are arranged in roughly spherical heads on the ends of branches which continue to grow after flowering. The flowers have 5 bundles of stamens. The stamens are joined for most of their length, with about 3 separate filaments extending beyond the joined part. Some bundles are more than 19mm long while others in the same flower are much shorter. The variation in stamen length in the individual flowers is a distinguishing feature of this Beaufortia. Flowering occurs frequently but mostly from November to April, and is followed by fruit which are woody, up to 15mm long and 12mm wide; more or less clustered.

Taxonomy and naming

Beaufortia anisandra was first formally described in 1843 by Johannes Conrad Schauer in *Dissertatio phytographica de Regelia, Beaufortia et Calothamno*. The specific epithet ("anisandra") is from the Ancient Greek *ánisos* meaning "unequal and *andrós* meaning "male

Distribution and habitat

Beaufortia anisandra mainly occurs South of Perth near the Stirling Range and as far East as the Fitzgerald River National Park. It grows in sand, rocky quartzite soils on hills, rocky outcrops and plains.

Beaufortia bicolor Strid

Badgingarra Beaufortia

Description

Beaufortia bicolor is a densely branched shrub which grows to a height of about 1 m and about 0.5 m wide. The leaves are arranged in opposite pairs and sessile. They are up to 10 mm long and 5mm wide, usually hairy and 3 – 5 veined.

The flowers are red, orange and yellow and are arranged in dense heads on the ends of branches which continue to grow after flowering. Interspersed between the flowers are tufts of white hairs. The flowers have 5 bundles of stamens. The stamens are usually yellow to orange in the lower half with red ends and are joined for about half their length. Flowering occurs throughout the year but mainly from October to January, and is followed by fruit which are woody capsules, arranged in small clusters around the stem.

Taxonomy and naming

Beaufortia bicolor was first formally described in 1987 by the Swedish botanist, Arne Strid in *Plant Systematics and Evolution* from a specimen found near Badgingarra.

Distribution and habitat

B. bicolor occurs primarily north of Jurien Bay. It grows on sandplains in white sand over laterite.

Authors Note: *I found this plant very difficult to locate because known locations are few, and flowering period was not clearly defined. It took me three visits north of Perth to find good flowering specimens.*

Conservation

Beaufortia bicolor is classified as "Priority Three" by the Western Australian Government Department of Parks and Wildlife meaning that it is known from only a few locations but is not under imminent threat.

25

Beaufortia bracteosa Diels

Description

Beaufortia bracteosa is a compact shrub growing to a height of about 1 m and about 0.5 m in diameter. The leaves are arranged in opposite pairs and are linear in shape, about 4mm long, 1.5 mm wide and generally ciliate but sometimes glabrous. The flowers are arranged in heads on the ends of the branches and have 5 bundles of stamens. They are deep pink to red or maroon. Flowering occurs throughout the year but especially in spring and early summer and is followed by fruit which are woody capsules to about 11 mm long and 6 mm wide.

Taxonomy and naming

Beaufortia bracteosa was first formally described in 1904 by Ludwig Diels in *Fragmenta Phytographiae Australiae occidentalis*. The specific epithet (*bracteosa*) is derived from the Latin word *bractea* meaning "scale" and the suffix -*osa* meaning "having many (or large) bracts.

Distribution and habitat

This Beaufortia grows in sandy soils, sometimes with clay, gravel or loam often over laterite or granite. It is widespread – found near Wongan Hills, Hyden, Jitarning, Brookton, Pingelly and Dumbleyung.It is an important component of heath and low shrubland. (Kwongan) vegetation.

Note: Can sometimes be confused with B. kwongkanicola, which has a larger, red inflorescence.

B. bracteosa is also closely related to B. purpurea, but has smaller leaves.

Beaufortia burbidgeae A.A.Burb. Column Beaufortia

Description

Beaufortia burbidgeae is a shrub which grows to a height of around 1m and about the same width. The leaves are needle-like, up to10 mm long and crowded on the woody stems. The flowers are arranged in heads on the ends of the branches and on short side branches.

The flowers have 5 bundles of stamens. The stamen bundles are deep red at their bases and pale green or pink on the ends, and hairy on the inner surface. There are 3 to 5 stamens in each bundle and the free ends of the stamens are a further 3–6 mm long. Flowering occurs mostly in spring and early summer. It is followed by fruit which are woody capsules that are sometimes seen in clusters.

Taxonomy and naming

Beaufortia burbidgeae was first formally described in 2016 by Andrew A. Burbidge and the description was published in *Nuytsia*. The specific epithet ("burbidgeae") honours Nancy Tyson Burbidge, the aunt of the author.

Distribution and habitat

Column Beaufortia grows in or near laterite on hills in heath and woodland, occasionally in sand. It has been primarily recorded in a reserve near Brookton.

Authors Note: *I visited the primary site three times without success, eventually finding it in Perth's Kings Park!*

Conservation

Beaufortia burbidgeae is classified as "Priority Three" by the Western Australian Government Department of Parks and Wildlife, meaning that even though it is known from only a few locations, it is not under imminent threat.

Beaufortia cyrtodonta (Turcz.) Benth. Stirling Range Bottlebrush

Description

Beaufortia cyrtodonta is a compact shrub which grows to a height of 1.5 meters.

The leaves are linear to lance-shaped, up to 7 mm long and often have a covering of fine hairs, giving them a greyish appearance.

The inflorescences are red and are arranged in heads about 2.5 mm in diameter on the ends of branches. The flowers have 5 bundles of stamens. Flowering occurs from June to November and is followed by fruits which are woody capsules about 10 mm long and clustered together.

Taxonomy and naming

B. cyrtodonta was first formally described in 1867 by Nikolai Turczaninow in *Bulletin de la Societe Imperiale des Naturalistes de Moscou* as Melaleuca cyrtodonta. In 1867, George Bentham transferred it to *Beaufortia* as *Beaufortia cyrtodonta* The specific epithet ("cyrtodonta") is from the Ancient Greek *kyrtos* meaning "curved" or "bent "and *odontos* meaning "toothed".

Distribution and habitat

Beaufortia cyrtodonta mainly occurs in the Stirling Range, but has been recorded east of Lake Grace... It grows in sandy or stony soils occasionally in sandheath or open woodland.

Beaufortia decussata R.Br. Gravel Bottlebrush

Description

Beaufortia decussata is an erect, open shrub with few branches growing to a height of 3m...

The leaves are arranged in alternating pairs. They are egg-shaped, pointed at the end, about 10mm long and usually have 5 veins visible.

The flowers are red to orange red and are arranged in bottlebrush-like spikes about 40mm in diameter and 100mm long, forming a cylinder around the long stems under their branches. There are 5 small petals and 5 bundles of stamens which give the flowers their colour and are much longer than the inconspicuous petals. Flowering occurs all year around and is followed by fruit which are woody capsules.

Taxonomy and naming

B. decussata was the first species of *Beaufortia* to be described. It was formally described in 1812 by Robert Brown in William Townsend Aiton's *Hortus Kewensis*. The specific epithet ("decussata") is from the Latin *decusso* meaning "arranged crosswise or marked with a cross".

Distribution and habitat

Beaufortia decussata is widespread in the South-West, found in the Stirling Ranges, Albany, Denmark, Pemberton, and Walpole & Nornalup. It grows in sandy soils, lateritic gravel and occasionally in swampy ground.

Beaufortia elegans Schauer

Elegant Beaufortia

Description

Beaufortia elegans is an erect, usually spreading shrub which can grow to a height of 2.5 metres.

The leaves are arranged in opposite pairs and are 2–5 mm long, crowded, dished, curved and lacking a stalk.

The flowers are usually red to dark purplish red but other colours and white flowers are sometimes seen. They are arranged in heads about 20 mm in diameter, on the ends of branches which continue to grow after flowering. The flowers have 5 bundles of stamens. Each bundle contains 4 to 7 stamens joined for about 3–4 mm long of their length with the free parts a further 4–6 mm long. Flowering occurs mostly from October to December and is followed by fruits which are woody, almost spherical capsules 8–10 mm in diameter.

Taxonomy and naming

Beaufortia elegans was first formally described in 1843 by Johannes Conrad Schauer in *Dissertatio phytographica de Regelia, Beaufortia et Calothamno*. The specific epithet ("elegans") is a Latin word meaning "fine", "choice" or "tasteful".

Distribution and habitat

Beaufortia elegans mainly occurs in the vicinity of Three Springs, Wongan Hills, Carnamah and Eneabba. It usually grows in sand amongst heath & low shrubland, often over laterite on plains and in areas that are wet in winter.

Beaufortia empetrifolia (Rchb.) Schauer South Coast Beaufortia

Description

Beaufortia empetrifolia is a compact, much branched shrub which grows to a height of 2m. The leaves are arranged in opposite pairs.

The leaves are egg-shaped, 1.5–3mm long and 0.5–2mm wide.

The flowers are pink to purplish red and are arranged in heads about 20mm in diameter, on the ends of branches which continue to grow after flowering. The flowers have 5 bundles of stamens with usually three to five stamens each. The stamens bundles are hairy and joined for 1.5–5mm of their length with the free parts a further 2.5–5mm long. Flowering can occur in almost any month, depending on the weather and is followed by fruits which are woody capsules. The capsules are 6.5–11.5mm long and 5–6mm wide and often joined together.

Taxonomy and naming

B. empetrifolia was first formally described in 1828 by the German botanist, Ludwig Reichenbach in *Iconographia Botanica Exotica as Melaleuca empetrifolia*. In 1843, Johannes Schauer recognised it as *Beaufortia empetrifolia*.

The specific epithet ("empetrifolia") refers to *Empetrum*, a genus of plants in the Family Ericaceae and *folia*, the plural of the Latin word *folium* meaning "a leaf".

Distribution and habitat

Beaufortia empetrifolia has been recorded as being found between Albany and Esperance; South Stirlings, Bremer Bay, Fitzgerald River National Park and Cape Arid National Park. It usually grows in sand, often near granite outcrops.

Beaufortia eriocephala W.Fitzg. Woolly Bottlebrush

Description

Beaufortia eriocephala is a compact shrub which grows to a height of 0.5m and 0.4m wide.

The leaves are arranged in opposite pairs and are linear to narrowly lance-shaped, 5–10mm long and 0.4–0.7mm wide. The leaves are hairy but become glabrous with age. Appears related to B. purpurea but the leaves are more ciliate.

The flowers are arranged in almost spherical heads on the ends of branches which continue to grow after flowering. The flowers have 5 bundles of stamens. The stamen bundles contain 3 to 5 stamens each, with the joined part deep red, hairy and 2.5–3.5mm long. The free part of the stamens is red to purple and a further 3–4.5mm long.

Flowering occurs from October to December and is followed by fruits which are woody capsules 8.5–10mm long.

Taxonomy and naming

Beaufortia eriocephala was first formally described in 1905 by the Australian botanist, William Vincent Fitzgerald in *Journal of the West Australian Natural History Society*. The specific epithet ("eriocephala") is from the Ancient Greek *(érion)* meaning "wool" and *(kephalḗ)* meaning "head".

Distribution and habitat

Beaufortia eriocephala occurs near Badgingarra, growing in sand and lateritic soil.

Conservation
Beaufortia eriocephala is classified Priority 3 – known from only a few locations but is not under iminent threat.

Beaufortia incana (Benth.) A.S.George Grey-leaved Beaufortia

Description

Beaufortia incana is a compact shrub which grows to a height of 2m. The leaves are arranged alternately; crowded on the younger stems, linear to lance-shaped and arranged in alternate pairs. The leaves are about 6.5–10.5mm long and have a covering of fine hairs on both surfaces, but very variable.

The flowers are red and arranged in dense heads about of 25mm in diameter on the ends of the branches, and are surrounded by long soft hairs. The flowers have 5 bundles of stamens.

The stamens give the flowers their colour and are in bundles of 3, joined for most of their variable length. Flowering occurs from August to December and is followed by fruit which are woody capsules.

Taxonomy and naming

Beaufortia incana was first formally described in 1867 by George Bentham in *Flora Australiensis* as *Beaufortia macrostemon var. Incana*.

In 1972, Alex George raised it to species status in Nuytsia. The specific epithet ("incana") is a Latin word meaning "quite gray".

Distribution and habitat

Beaufortia incana is widespread – locations include Popanyinning, Tutanning Reserve, Dryandra State Forest and Boyagin Nature Reserve. It grows in sandy and lateritic soils.

Beaufortia kwongkanicola A.A.Burb.

Lesueur Beaufortia

Description

Beaufortia kwongkanicola is a shrub which grows to a height and width of 1m. The leaves are arranged in opposite pairs, are linear to narrow egg-shaped, 3–8mm long, 1–2.5mm wide and are often crowded

The flowers are arranged in heads on the ends of the branches and have 5 bundles of stamens. The stamen bundles are deep red to purple, 3–8mm long and densely hairy on the inner surface.

There are 5 to 7 stamens in each bundle and the free ends of the stamens separate from the bundle at different points. Flowering occurs from July to November and is followed by fruit which are woody capsules, 10–13mm long and about 8mm wide and densely clustered.

Taxonomy and naming

Beaufortia kwongkanicola was first formally described in 2016 by Andrew A. Burbidge and the description was published in *Nuytsia*. The specific epithet ("kwongkanicola") refers to the kwongkan – heath and low shrubland in which this species is found.

It has been confused with both B. bracteosa and B. eriocephala in the past.

Distribution and habitat

Lesueur Beaufortia grows in sandy soils often over laterite.

It has been recorded north of Perth in Badgingarra, Eneabba and North-west of Watheroo.

Beaufortia macrostemon Lindl. Darling Range Beaufortia

Description

Beaufortia macrostemon is a low shrub with multiple branches at the base, about 0.5m high, but occasionally taller. Its leaves are arranged in opposite pairs, linear to lance-shaped, 10–12mm long, 1–2mm wide and hairy, at least when young. It is one of the few Beaufortias with a lignotuber.

The flowers are mostly red and are arranged in heads on the ends of the branches. There are five bundles of stamens. The stamen bundles are pale yellow brown to red, 7–12mm long and hairy near the base. There are 3 stamens in each bundle and the free parts are bright red, 3–7mm and separate at a single point. Flowering occurs from September to January and is followed by fruit which are woody capsules, 10mm long and wide, joined in bundles.

Taxonomy and naming

Beaufortia macrostemon was first formally described in 1839 by the English botanist John Lindley in *A Sketch of the Vegetation of the Swan River Colony*. The specific epithet (*macrostemon*) is derived from the Ancient Greek *makros* meaning "large" or "long" and *stemon* meaning "thread" or "filament".

Distribution and habitat

This Beaufortia usually grows in lateritic soil and is most abundant on the Darling Scarp in Jarrah forest.

Beaufortia micrantha Schauer Little Bottlebrush

Description

Beaufortia micrantha is a small, compact shrub which grows to a height of about 0.5 metres but sometimes taller.

The leaves are triangular in shape with the end tapering to a point, 1–2 mm long and have their upper surfaces pressed against the stems, sometimes overlapping each other.

The flowers are usually pinkish-red to purple and are arranged in heads about 10 mm in diameter, 15 mm long on the ends of branches which continue to grow after flowering. The flowers have 5 bundles of stamens. The stamen bundles have 3 to 5 stamens each, are 6–10 mm long with the free parts a further 5–10 mm long. Flowering occurs in most months but mainly from September to November and is followed by fruits which are woody capsules 25–35 mm long, 6–10 mm wide and closely packed together'.

Taxonomy and naming

Beaufortia micrantha was first formally described in 1843 by Johannes Conrad Schauer in *Dissertatio phytographica de Regelia, Beaufortia et Calothamno*. The specific epithet (*micrantha*) is derived from the Ancient Greek *mikrós* meaning "small" and *ánthos* meaning "flower".

Distribution and habitat

Beaufortia micrantha occurs south between Albany and Esperance and north to the Corrigin & Southern Cross areas. It usually grows in sandy soils, or sand mixed with laterite.

Beaufortia orbifolia F.Muell. Ravensthorpe Bottlebrush

Description

Beaufortia orbifolia is an erect, sometimes open, spreading shrub which grows to a height of about 3m. The leaves are arranged in alternate pairs (decussate). The leaves are flat or slightly dished, broad egg-shaped to round, 4.5–6mm long and have 5 or 7 veins.

The flowers are red and green and are arranged in bottlebrush-like spikes about 40mm in diameter and 60mm long on the ends of branches which continue to grow after flowering. The flowers have 5 bundles of stamens. The stamen bundles contain 3 to 7 stamens, are green in their lower half and red in the upper half and joined for about half of their length. Flowering occurs from August to January, but has been recorded as in flower all year round. It is followed by fruits which are woody capsules in roughly spherical or cylindrical clusters.

Taxonomy and naming

Beaufortia orbifolia was first formally described in 1862 by Victorian government botanist, Ferdinand von Mueller in Fragmenta phytographiae Australiae from a specimen collected on the slopes of East Mount Barren by George Maxwell The specific epithet (*orbifolia*) is derived from the Latin *orbis* meaning "a circle" and *folium* meaning "a leaf".

Distribution and habitat

Beaufortia orbifolia is widespread near Ravensthorpe and in the Fitzgerald River National Park.

It usually grows in sandy soils, sand over laterite and sometimes in sand.

Beaufortia puberula Turcz.

Hairy-leaved Beaufortia

Description

Beaufortia puberula is a shrub which grows to a height of 2m and sometimes spreading to 2m wide. The leaves are arranged in opposite pairs and are 1.5–4mm long &1–1.5mm wide and hairy.

The flowers are pink or deep pink to red and are arranged in heads on the ends of the branches.

The flowers have 5 bundles of stamens. The stamen bundles are about 1–3mm long with 5 to7 separate stamen filaments a further 1–2.5mm long. The inner surface of the bundles is glabrous, the outer face is covered with long hairs. Flowering occurs in most months and is followed by fruit which are woody capsules 10–16mm long and about 5mm in diameter, joined in cluster.

Taxonomy and naming

Beaufortia puberula was first formally described in 1852 by Nikolai Turczaninow and the description was published in *Bulletin de la Classe Physico-Mathématique de l'Académie Impériale des Sciences de Saint-Pétersbourg*. The specific epithet (*puberula*) is derived from a Latin word meaning "downy" The species had previously been known as *Beaufortia interstans, and was referred to by Bentham in Flora Australiaensis, as B. micrantha var perberula.*

Distribution and habitat

Hairy leaved Beaufortia grows in sandy soil and sandy loam, often over laterite or sandy, lateritic gravel, east & south east of Perth – has been recorded in the vicinity of a number of Towns including Hyden, Dumbleyung, and Merredin & Tammin.

Have included an image of a dried and mounted specimen of B.puberula from the Western Australian Herbarium.

Beaufortia purpurea Lindl. Purple Beaufortia

Description

Beaufortia purpurea is an erect, sometimes open, spreading shrub with long, straight, thin branches and which grows to a height of about 1.5m. The leaves are arranged in alternate pairs (decussate) on the branches, the older leaves are lance shaped to egg shaped, up to 10 mm long and 5mm wide with 3 to 5 veins and glabrous.

The flowers are purple or purplish red and are arranged in bottlebrush-like spikes on the ends of branches which continue to grow after flowering. The flowering part of the stem is densely hairy and the flowers have 5 bundles of stamens. These bundles, give the flowers their colour. They contain 3 to 7 stamens (mostly 5) which are joined for about half their length. Flowering mainly occurs from September to December and is followed by fruit which are woody capsules in clusters about 12mm long.

Taxonomy and naming

Beaufortia purpurea was first formally described in 1839 by English botanist, John Lindley in "A Sketch of the Vegetation of the Swan River Colony". The specific epithet ("purpurea") is a Latin word meaning "purple".

Distribution and habitat

Beaufortia purpurea mainly occurs in the outer suburbs of Perth in the Jarrah Forest in small conservation Reserves of the Darling Scarp.

It usually grows in soils derived from laterite or granite on rocky slopes.

Conservation

Beaufortia purpurea is classified as "**Priority Three**" by the Western Australian Government Department of Parks and Wildlife meaning that it is known from only a few locations but is not under imminent threat.

Beaufortia raggedensis A.A.Burb. Mount Ragged Beaufortia

Description

Beaufortia raggedensis is usually a compact shrub, sometimes openly branched, which grows to a height of 1.5 metres. The leaves are arranged in opposite pairs and are linear in shape, 5–10 mm long, less than 1 mm wide and are often in dense clusters. They often have a covering of fine hairs, giving them a greyish appearance.

The flowers are deep red and are arranged in heads on the ends of branches. They have 5 bundles of stamens. The bundles contain between 5 and 7 stamens and are joined for 5–10 mm with the free stamens branching at different points. Flowering occurs from September to December and is followed by fruits which are woody capsules and joined together.

Taxonomy and naming

Beaufortia raggedensis was first formally described in 2016 by Andrew A. Burbidge and the description was published in *Nuytsia*. The specific epithet ("raggedensis") refers to Mount Ragged, in Cape Arid National Park, east of Esperance; where this species is found.

Distribution and habitat

Beaufortia raggedensis grows in quartzite, only on the slopes of the Russell Range in the Cape Arid National Park.

Conservation

Beaufortia raggedensis is classified as "Priority Two" by the Western Australian Government Department of Parks and Wildlife meaning that it is poorly known and from one only, or a few locations.

Photos courtesy: Mary Hoggart

Beaufortia schaueri Schauer Pink Beaufortia

Description

Beaufortia schaueri is a small, compact shrub which grows to a height of about 1.5 metres & about 1.2 metres wide.

The leaves are arranged in alternating pairs. They are about 6 mm long, sessile, linear and glabrous in appearance.

The flowers are bright pink to mauve and are arranged in almost spherical heads on the ends of branches which continue to grow after flowering. The flowers have 5 bundles of stamens. There are usually 5 stamens per bundle and they are joined for about half their length. Flowering is almost all year round but primarily in spring and summer followed by fruits which are woody capsules.

Taxonomy

Beaufortia schaueri was first formally described in 1843 by Johannes Conrad Schauer in Dissertatio phytographica de Regelia, Beaufortia et Calothamno.

Distribution and habitat

Beaufortia schaueri is widespread, broadly found between Albany and Esperance. It usually grows in sandy soils or those derived from laterite on plains and slopes.

Beaufortia sparsa R.Br. Swamp Bottlebrush

Description

Beaufortia sparsa is an evergreen shrub that grows to approximately 3 metres tall and 2 metres wide. The leaves are described as bright green, spiraled, ovate to lanceolate; 7mm-10mm long and 3mm-4mm wide.

The flowers are bright orange to red in colour and arranged in bottlebrush-like spikes near the ends of the branches that continue to grow after flowering. The flowers have 5 bundles of stamens each containing about 5 stamens. The stamens, which give the flowers their colour, are up to 26 mm long. Flowers are produced primarily from January to May but can be seen throughout the year. They are followed by fruits which are woody capsules and retained on the stems indefinitely.

Taxonomy and naming

Beaufortia sparsa was first formally described in 1812 by Scottish botanist, Robert Brown in William Aiton's Hortus Kewensis. The specific epithet ("sparsa") is a Latin word meaning "scattered".

Distribution and habitat

Beaufortia sparsa mainly occurs between Busselton and Albany.

It usually grows in sand in swampy places or near watercourses.

Use in horticulture

Swamp bottlebrush is probably the most widely cultivated in the genus *Beaufortia* but it is not well known in gardens. It is difficult to grow in the more humid eastern states but in drier climates is a colourful feature.

Beaufortia sprengelioides (DC.) Craven
Shark Bay Beaufortia

Description

Beaufortia sprengelioides is a rigid, spreading shrub which grows to a height of about 2 metres. The leaves are crowded and mostly arranged in alternate pairs so that, especially on the younger branches, they make four rows along the stems. The leaves are flat or slightly dished, broad egg-shaped to round, 2–3 mm long and have 3 veins, not including the marginal veins.

The flowers are pale pink to white and arranged in spherical heads on the ends of branches which continue to grow after flowering. The flowers have 5 bundles of stamens. The stamen bundles, which give the flowers their colour, contain 9 to 15 stamens and are joined for more than half their length. Flowering occurs from July to November and is followed by fruits which are woody capsules.

Taxonomy and naming

Beaufortia sprengelioides was collected before 1670 by the English explorer, William Dampier. It was first formally described in 1828 by the Swiss botanist, Augustin de Candolle in Prodromus Systematis Naturalis Regni Vegetabilis and given the name *Melaleuca sprengelioides*. Schauer then included de Candolle's plant in *Regelia ciliata*, apparently on the basis of de Candolle's drawings. In 1999, Lyndley Craven reinterpreted Schauer's work and gave the plant the name *Beaufortia sprengelioides*. The specific epithet ("sprengelioides") is a reference to the genus *Sprengelia* in the family Ericaceae.

Distribution and habitat

Beaufortia sprengelioides mainly occurs between Geraldton and Shark Bay, and includes nearby off-shore islands. It usually grows in sand, over laterite and limestone.

Beaufortia squarrosa Schauer Sand Beaufortia

Description

Beaufortia squarrosa is a shrub which grows to a height of about 2 metres. The leaves are crowded and arranged in alternating pairs; they are egg-shaped to oval, less than 4.5 mm long and have 5 to 7 veins.

The flowers are usually bright red but sometimes orange or yellow and are arranged in roughly spherical heads on the ends of branches which continue to grow after flowering. The flowers have 5 bundles of stamens. The stamen bundles, which give the flower its colour, contain 3 to 7 stamens and are joined for more than half their length. Flowering occurs mostly in spring and summer, but will flower much of the year. The flowers are followed by fruits which are woody capsules.

Taxonomy and naming

Beaufortia squarrosa was first formally described in 1843 by Johannes Conrad Schauer in Dissertatio phytographica de Regelia, Beaufortia et Calothamno.The specific epithet ("squarrosa") is a Latin word meaning "scurfy" or "scabby".

Distribution and habitat

Beaufortia squarrosa mainly occurs on the coastal plain between Busselton and Eneabba, and further north to Alexander Morrison National Park. It grows predominantly in sandy soils which may be either dry or winter-wet.

Eremaea

Eremaea beaufortioides

Eremaea blackwelliana

Eremaea acutifolia F.Muell. Rusty Eremaea

Description

Eremaea acutifolia is an erect to spreading shrub which sometimes grows to a height of 0.7 metres and which, unlike some others in the genus, lacks a lignotuber. The leaves are linear to narrow elliptic in shape, 3.6–9.5 mm long, 0.5–1.2 mm wide and have a single prominent vein visible on the lower surface.

The flowers are usually orange and are often found on the ends of short side branches off the previous year's wood. The flowers occur singly, rarely two together. The stamens are arranged in 5 bundles, each containing 28 to 34 stamens. Flowering occurs from August to November and is followed by fruits which are woody capsules. The capsules are shaped like an inverted cone and are rough or lumpy on the outer surface.

Taxonomy and naming

Eremaea acutifolia was first formally described in 1860 by Ferdinand von Mueller in Fragmenta Phytographiae Australiae. The specific epithet (*acutifolia*) is from the Latin *acutus* meaning "sharp" or "pointed" and *folium* meaning "a leaf" referring to the pointed leaves of this species.

Distribution and habitat

Eremaea acutifolia is only found in a small area east of Geraldton.

It grows in sand on sandplains.

Conservation

Eremaea acutifolia is classified as "Priority three" by the Western Australian Government Department of Parks and Wildlife. This means that it is only known from a few locations but is not under imminent threat.

Eremaea asterocarpa Hnatiuk

Description

Eremaea asterocarpa is a shrub, growing to a height of 1.3 metres. It has a variable form, sometimes low and spreading, others erect or short and twisted. The leaves are 3.4–8.3 mm long, 1.0–4.5 mm wide, elliptic or egg-shaped with the narrower end towards the base and have between 5 and 7 veins visible on the lower surface.

The flowers are orange-coloured, on the ends of the previous year's wood and occur singly and occasionally two together. There are 5 sepals which are densely hairy on the outside surface and 5 petals; the stamens, which give the flower its orange colour, are arranged in bundles of five, each containing 16 to 36 stamens. Flowering occurs from July to November and is followed by fruits which are woody capsules. The capsules are more or less cup-shaped, rough and lumpy with the remains of the sepals giving a star-like appearance. It can be distinguished from other eremaeas by the rough fruits and the presence of 5 or more veins on the leaves.

Taxonomy and naming

Eremaea asterocarpa was first formally described in 1993 by Roger Hnatiuk in Nuytsia. The specific epithet (*asterocarpa*) refers to the "star-fruit"

There are three subspecies of Eremaea asterocarpa:

- Eremaea asterocarpa subsp. asterocarpa Hnatiuk has leaves with 3 to 5 veins.
- Eremaea asterocarpa subsp. histoclada Hnatiuk is an erect plant with straight or slightly arched branches and leaves with 5 to 7 or more veins.
- Eremaea asterocarpa subsp. brachyclada Hnatiuk is a small, low shrub with short, twisted branches and leaves with 5 to 7 or more veins.

Distribution and habitat

Eremaea asterocarpa is found in near-coastal areas of the south-west Jarrah Forest and Swan Coastal Plain - Jurien to Perth. It grows in sand over laterite.

Conservation

Eremaea asterocarpa is classified as "not threatened" by the W.A. Govt. Dept. of Parks and Wildlife, however a small population of E.asterocarpa has been recorded in an outer southern suburb of Perth. This area, is presently undergoing extensive medium density residential development.

69

Eremaea poss. atala Hnatiuk

Description

Eremaea atala is a small, erect shrub with spreading branches, growing to a height of 1.2 metres. The leaves are 7.3–10 mm long, 0.8–1.5 mm wide, flat, narrow egg-shaped with the narrower end towards the base and have a single vein visible on the lower surface. Unlike some others in the genus, the leaves are soft and not prickly.

The flowers are purple/mauve coloured and arranged in groups of generally three in the angles of the leaves, mostly along the current year's growth. There are 5 sepals which are densely hairy on the outside surface and 5 petals. The stamens, which give the flower its colour, are arranged in bundles of 5, each containing 19 to 20 stamens. Flowering occurs from November to January and is followed by fruits which are woody capsules. The capsules are more or less cup-shaped and smooth.

Taxonomy and naming

Eremaea atala was first formally described in 1993 by Roger Hnatiuk in Nuytsia. The specific epithet (*atala*) is from the Greek, *atalos* meaning "soft" or "delicate", referring to the soft leaves of this species compared to those of the closely related Eremaea violacea and E. hadra.

Distribution and habitat

Eremaea atala is found between Northampton and Eneabba – north of Perth. It grows in sand over laterite.

Eremaea beaufortioides Benth.

Description

Its leaves are about 3mm–6 mm long, 1.5mm–4 mm wide, flat, linear to broad egg-shaped and with up to 7 veins sometimes visible on the lower surface. There is variation in leaf size and shape between the three varieties of the species.

The flowers are orange-coloured and arranged in groups of up to six on the ends of the branches of the previous year's growth. The stamens, which give the flower its colour, are arranged in 5 bundles, each containing 34 to 48 stamens. Flowering occurs from September to December and is followed by fruits which are woody capsules. The capsules are more or less barrel-shaped and smooth.

Taxonomy and naming

Eremaea beaufortioides was first formally described in 1867 by George Bentham in Flora Australiensis.

There are three varieties:

- *Eremaea beaufortioides* var. *beaufortioides* has thin leaves with 5 or more veins and flowers with a glabrous hypanthium.
- *Eremaea beaufortioides* var. *lachnostanthe* has thin leaves with 3 veins and flowers with a densely hairy hypanthium.
- *Eremaea beaufortioides* var. *microphylla* has small, thick leaves with fewer than 3 veins which may be hard to see.

Distribution and habitat

Eremaea beaufortioides is widespread between Geraldton and Perth.

It grows in sand over laterite.

Use in horticulture

Eremaea beaufortioides is an attractive species but although it is the hardiest of its Genus, is difficult to grow in more humid areas unless grafted. It needs a sunny position and excellent drainage.

Eremaea blackwelliana Hnatiuk

Description

Eremaea blackwelliana is a shrub with spreading branches, growing to about 1.5 metres high and can be up to 3 m wide. The leaves are 8.8–9.7 mm long, 0.6–0.9 mm wide, linear, pointed but not sharp and are thickened along the mid-line.

The flowers are orange-coloured and occur singly on the end of branches formed the previous year. The outer surface of the flower cup (the hypanthium) is densely hairy. There are 5 petals to 4 mm long. The stamens, which give the flower its colour, are arranged in 5 bundles, each containing 20 to 26 stamens. My research indicated that the flowering period was from September to November, followed by fruits which are woody capsules. The capsules are more or less cup-shaped to spherical and smooth.

Taxonomy and naming

E. blackwelliana was first formally described in 1993 by Roger Hnatiuk in Nuytsia. The specific epithet (*blackwelliana*) honours Marion Blackwell, a landscape designer who encouraged the cultivation of Australian native plants.

Distribution and habitat

Eremaea blackwelliana is found near Toodyay, north-east of Perth. It grows in sand in gently sloping depressions. The Toodyay location is fairly wet.

Conservation

E. blackwelliana is listed as "Priority 4" by the Western Australian Government Department of Parks and Wildlife meaning that it is rare and endangered.

Authors Note: *I found this Eremaea in one location only. There was a second location recorded, but I was unable to find it. I also found that the flowering period cited was inaccurate. It was necessary, to visit the primary location three times before successfully obtaining images of this Eremaea in flower*

75

Eremaea brevifolia (Benth.) Domin

Description

Eremaea brevifolia is an erect, densely foliaged to spreading shrub; which sometimes grows to a height of 1.5 metres. The leaves are 4 -7mm long, 3–6 mm wide, flat, crowded and so that they overlap each other. They are broadly egg-shaped with the narrower end towards the base and have 5 to 9 veins visible on the lower surface.

The flowers are orange-coloured, 8–10 mm across and (usually) occur singly on the end of short branches which grew the previous year. There are 5 sepals which are densely hairy on the outside surface and 5 petals. The stamens are arranged in bundles of 5, each containing 50 to 70 stamens. Flowering occurs from August to October and is followed by fruits which are woody capsules. The capsules are cup-shaped and rough or lumpy on the outer surface. The leaves and fruits of this species are similar to those of *Eremaea asterocarpa* but the bracts surrounding the flowers are hairy.

Taxonomy and naming

Eremaea brevifolia was first formally described in 1923 by the Czech botanist Karel Domin in Vestnik Kralovske Ceske Spolecnosti Nauk, Trida Matematiko-Prirodevedecke. It had previously been known as a variety of *Eremaea fimbriata* - E. fimbriata var. *brevifolia* Benth. The specific epithet (*brevifolia*) is from the Latin *brevis* meaning "short" and *folium* meaning "a leaf" referring to the short leaves of this species compared to the subspecies now called *Eremaea asterocarpa* subsp. *asterocarpa*.

Distribution and habitat

Eremaea brevifolia is recorded as occurring in the Geraldton Sandplains between Geraldton and Kalbarri, north of Perth. It grows in sand or laterite on plains and rock outcrops.

Authors Note: *It was pure luck that I located this species. The locations I was aware of were unsuccessful. I spotted this one plant amongst vegetation above one of the main roads into Geraldton on an elevated ridge.*

Eremaea ×*codonocarpa* Hnatiuk

Description

Eremaea × *codonocarpa* is usually an erect shrub, but sometimes prostrate; growing to a height of about 0.7 meter. The leaves are 4–11 mm long, 0.6–2 mm wide, linear to narrow egg-shaped tapering to a point and more or less triangular in cross section. They have a covering of fine hairs and one to three veins on the lower surface.

The flowers are pink to deep pink and occur in small groups (usually pairs) on the end of short branches from longer ones formed the previous year. The outer surface of the flower cup is densely hairy. There are 5 petals. The stamens, which give the flower its colour, are arranged in 5 bundles, each containing 19 to 26 stamens. Flowering occurs from October to November and is followed by fruits which are woody capsules. The capsules are more or less urn-shaped, with a rough, flaky surface.

Taxonomy and naming

Eremaea × *codonocarpa* was first formally described in 1993 in the Nuytsia Journal from a specimen found near Jurien Bay. Hnatiuk considers *Eremaea* × *codonocarpa* to be a stabilised hybrid between *E. asterocarpa* subsp. *asterocarpa* and *E. violacea* subsp. *raphiophylla*. The name *codonocarpa* is derived from the Greek word *kódon* meaning "bell" and *karpós* meaning "fruit", alluding to the urn-shaped or bell-shaped fruits.

Distribution and habitat

Eremaea × *codonocarpa* occurs in the Geraldton Sandplains – between Jurien Bay and Dongara, north of Perth. It grows in sandy laterite on sandplains.

Authors Note: *I found this plant (1 of 2) on the last day of one of my field trips. I had visited all the locations I was aware of and was going to give this one a miss. However, before heading home I decided to backtrack and visit this location one last time. Thank goodness I did!*

Eremaea dendroidea Hnatiuk

Description

Eremaea dendroidea is a shrub or small tree, growing to a height of 3.5 metres. Its branches point upwards from the main stem and the younger branches are densely covered with fine hairs. The leaves are 3–5 mm long, 0.7–2 mm wide, narrow elliptic or narrow egg-shaped, flat and glabrous. Sometimes there is a single vein visible on the lower surface.

The flowers are orange-coloured, on the ends of the long branches and occur singly or in pairs. There are 5 sepals which have a few hairs on the outside surface and 5 petals. The stamens, which give the flower its colour, are arranged in 5 bundles, each containing 46 to 49 stamens.

Flowering is supposed to occur only in September followed by fruits which are woody capsules. The capsules are smooth on the outer surface and more or less cup-shaped. However when we located these plants in mid-September, there was no indication that they were even close to flowering.

Unlike most others in the genus, the fruits of E.dendroidea open and release their seeds when they are mature and are not retained in the fruit until the death of the plant.

Taxonomy and naming

Eremaea dendroidea was first formally described in 1993 by Roger Hnatiuk in Nuytsia. The specific epithet (*dendroidea*) is from the Greek *(déndron)* meaning "a tree" and *(eîdos)* meaning "form" or "likeness" referring to the tree like growth form of this species.

Distribution and habitat

Eremaea dendroidea is found east of Geraldton near Mullewa, and further north. It grows in sandy soil on sand dunes.

Authors Note: *This Eremaea was very difficult to find. Two of the three locations I was aware of proved unsuccessful. A third location was successful, but there were only 2 or 3 specimens on a dangerous, sandy track near Mullewa. Once again, flowering times were inaccurate and it was necessary to go back several weeks later. It was 39deg.-41deg. on the particular day I returned, and I almost missed the plants. It was the end of their flowering period, swarming with flies with a strong easterly blowing – very difficult conditions to obtain good images.*

Eremaea ebracteata F.Muell.

Description

Eremaea ebracteata is a shrub which grows to a height of about 1 meter and which has its younger branches densely covered with fine hairs. The leaves are linear to broad egg-shaped with the narrower end towards to base, 2–8 mm long, up to 2 mm wide and have a single prominent vein visible on the lower surface.

The flowers are orange and are on the ends of long branches which grew earlier in the same season. The flowers occur singly, rarely two or three together. There are 5 sepals which are hairy on the outside surface and 5 petals. The stamens are arranged in bundles of 5, each containing 40 to 60 stamens. Flowering occurs from November to December and is followed by fruits which are woody capsules. The capsules are, cup shaped to almost spherical and are rough or lumpy on the outer surface.

Taxonomy and naming

Eremaea ebracteata was first formally described in 1860 by Ferdinand von Mueller in Fragmenta Phytographiae Australiae. The specific epithet (*ebracteata*) is from the Latin '*e*' meaning "without" and *bracteatus* meaning "gilt".

There are two varieties:

- *Eremaea ebracteata* F.Muell. Var. *ebracteata* has linear leaves 4–8 mm long, up to 1.0 mm wide.
- *Eremaea ebracteata* var. *brachyphylla* Hnatiuk has elliptic or egg-shaped leaves 2.5–3.0 mm long & 1.3–1.7 mm wide.
- The two varieties differ mainly in leaf size and shape.

Distribution and habitat

Eremaea ebracteata is found between Dongara and Kalbarri, north of Perth; however E. ebracteata var. *ebracteata,* generally occurs in more northern parts of the range. It grows in sand or sandy loam on sandplains.

Eremaea poss. ectadioclada Hnatiuk

Description

Eremaea ectadioclada is a low, spreading shrub growing to a height of 0.7 metres. Its younger branches are densely covered with fine hairs. The leaves are 4–10 mm long, 0.4–2.0 mm wide, narrow egg-shaped, tapering to a point. There is a single vein, sometimes three veins visible on the lower surface.

The flowers are orange-coloured and occur singly or in pairs, on the ends of the longer branches which grew in the previous year. There are 5 sepals which are densely covered with hairs on the outside surface and 5 petals 4–6 mm long. The stamens, which give the flower its colour, are arranged in 5 bundles, each containing 16 to 36 stamens. Flowering occurs from July to November and is followed by fruits which are woody capsules. The capsules are rough and scaly on the outer surface and more or less barrel-shaped or cup-shaped. This species can be distinguished from other Eremaeas by its rough, usually star-shaped fruit and narrow leaves.

Taxonomy and naming

Eremaea ectadioclada was first formally described in 1993 by Roger Hnatiuk in Nuytsia. The specific epithet (*ectadioclada*) is from the Ancient Greek *ektadios* meaning "spreading" and *klados* meaning "branch" in reference to the growth form of this species.

Distribution and habitat

Eremaea ectadioclada is found between Eneabba and Jurien Bay.

It grows in sandy soil over laterite on sandplains.

Conservation

Eremaea ectadioclada is classified as "not threatened" by the Western Australian Government Department of Parks and Wildlife.

Eremaea fimbriata Lindl.

Description

Eremaea fimbriata is a shrub growing to a height of about 1.0 meter. The leaves are narrow egg-shaped, tapering to a point and are 4–8 mm long, 0.5–4 mm wide and have one or three veins visible on the lower surface. There are a few long, soft hairs on the upper surface and the lower surface is densely covered with short, fine hairs.

The flowers are pink to deep pink and are borne singly on the ends of long branches which grew in the previous year. The flowers are 10–20 mm across and have 5 sepals which are densely hairy on the outside surface and have a short tuft of hairs on the top. The petals are 3–5 mm long.

The stamens are about 8 mm long are arranged in 5 bundles, each containing 13 to 18 stamens. Flowering occurs from July to September and is followed by fruits which are woody capsules. The capsules are 8.6–11 mm long, smooth and urn-shaped to almost spherical.

Taxonomy and naming

Eremaea fimbriata was first formally described in 1839 by John Lindley in A Sketch of the Vegetation of the Swan River Colony. The specific epithet (*fimbriata*) is from the Latin *fimbriatus* meaning "fringed".

Distribution and habitat

Eremaea fimbriata occurs in near-coastal areas north of Perth between Perth and Jurien. It grows in sandy soils, often with lateritic gravel.

Eremaea hadra Hnatiuk

Description

Eremaea hadra is a shrub growing to a height of 1.4 metres with erect branches and hairy younger branches. The leaves are thin, flat, 8–12 mm long, 1–3 mm wide, narrow elliptic in shape and taper to a sharp, prickly point. There is usually a single vein visible on the lower surface.

The flowers are deep violet and occur in groups of 2 to 9 on the ends of the longer branches which grew in the previous year or short ones of the latest growth. There are 5 sepals which are densely covered with hairs on the outside surface and 5 petals.

The stamens, which give the flower its colour, are arranged in 5 bundles, each containing 19 to 25 stamens. Flowering occurs from October to December and is followed by fruits which are woody capsules. The capsules are, smooth on the outer surface and cup-shaped or roughly spherical.

Taxonomy and naming

Eremaea hadra was first formally described in 1993 by Roger Hnatiuk in Nuytsia. The specific epithet (hadra) is from the Greek *'hadrós'* meaning "stout" or "strong".

Distribution and habitat

Eremaea hadra is found in the vicinity of Alexander Morrison National Park, north of Jurien Bay.

It grows in gravelly soil over laterite.

Authors Note: *I found this Eremaea very difficult find and to identify. It is very similar to Eremaea violacea subsp. raphiophylla. A lovely plant, nevertheless.*

Eremaea pauciflora (Endl.) Druce

Description

Eremaea pauciflora is an erect, spreading or densely foliaged and rounded shrub sometimes growing to a height of 2 metres. The leaves can be up to 8mm long & 3mm wide, linear to narrow egg-shaped with the narrower end towards the base. Sometimes 1 or 3 veins are visible on the lower surface.

The flowers are orange and are borne singly or sometimes in two's and three's, on the ends of long branches which grew in the previous year. The flowers have 5 sepals which are densely hairy on the outside surface and there are 5 petals. The stamens are arranged in 5 bundles, each containing 17 to 47 stamens. Flowering can occur from July to January and is followed by fruits which are woody capsules. The capsules are smooth and variable in shape.

Taxonomy and naming

E. pauciflora was originally known as *Metrosideros pauciflora*, having been formally described in 1837 by the Austrian botanist, Stephan Endlicher. The first species to be given the name *Eremaea* was *Eremaea fimbriata*, described in 1839 by John Lindley.

Eremaea pauciflora was formally described in 1917 by George Claridge Druce.

The specific epithet (*pauciflora*) is from ' *pauci'*- meaning few or little and '*flora* 'meaning "flowers".

There are three varieties:

- *Eremaea pauciflora* (Endl.) Druce var. *pauciflora* has linear leaves with 1 vein, fruits that have a very narrow opening and ranges throughout most of the south-west as well as the drier Coolgardie biogeographic region.
- *Eremaea pauciflora* var. *lonchophylla* Hnatiuk has narrow elliptic leaves with 1 or 3 veins and occurs in near-coastal areas between Perth and Geraldton
- *Eremaea pauciflora* var. *calyptra* Hnatiuk has linear leaves, cup-shaped fruit with a wide opening and occurs in near-coastal areas between Perth and Geraldton...

Distribution and habitat

Eremaea pauciflora is found throughout the south-west region of Western Australia – Geraldton to Albany. Its range also extends into the more arid areas of W.A. It is found in a wide range of habitats: sand, sandy clay on plains, on slopes and in winter-wet depressions.

Eremaea ×*phoenicea* Hnatiuk

Description

Eremaea × *phoenicea* is an erect, sometimes spreading shrub growing to a height of about 1.5 metres. The leaves are 4mm –7 mm long; up to 2 mm wide and are narrow elliptic to egg-shaped with the narrower end towards the base and the other end tapering to a point. They have a covering of fine hairs and one; sometimes three, veins on the lower surface.

The flowers are rose-colored to red and occur in groups of one to four on the end of branches formed the previous year. The outer surface of the flower cup - the hypanthium - is hairy and there are 5 petals. The stamens, which give the flower its colour, are arranged in 5 bundles, each containing 19 to 26 stamens. Flowering occurs from October to November and is followed by fruits which are woody capsules. The capsules are more or less urn-shaped with a smooth surface.

Taxonomy and naming

Eremaea × *phoenicea* was first formally described in 1993 in the Nuytsia Journal from a specimen found near Eneabba. Hnatiuk considers *Eremaea x phoenicea* to be a stabilised hybrid between *E. beaufortioides* and *E. violacea* subsp. *rhaphiophylla*.

The name *phoenicea* is derived from the Greek word *phoînix* meaning "purple" or "crimson" alluding to the flower colour of this species.

Distribution and habitat

Eremaea × *phoenicea* occurs in the Geraldton Sandplains where it grows in sand, in heath and low shrubland, generally between Jurien Bay and Eneabba, north of Perth.

Authors Note: *It was another memorable day when I found this lovely Eremaea. After a brief, albeit greasy, breakfast I headed off for my day of wildflower photography. As I got further away from my accommodation I started to feel distinctly uncomfortable. Nevertheless, I 'soldiered on' stopping a few times to obtain some images. I detoured down a surfaced road towards a Nature Reserve that I'd heard about, and was soon rewarded with some excellent flowering plants that I was looking for – this Eremaea was one of them. After crawling along a few more kilometers, stopping regularly for photographs, I really started to feel unwell, and began wondering if I was going to make it back to my accommodation in time? Fortunately, I soon arrived at a car park with some basic facilities. I was past caring about the numerous mosquitos and assorted other bugs everywhere; I didn't even care whether or not there were 'red-back's' under the toilet seat, I just had to sort myself out.*

From then on, for the rest of my field trips around the south-west I decided to have nothing for breakfast anywhere. Apart from coffee or tea!

Eremaea purpurea C.A.Gardner

Description

Eremaea purpurea is a shrub growing to a height of about 1.0 meter. The branches point upwards and the young stems are densely covered with hair. The leaves are narrow egg-shaped, tapering to a point and are up to 5 mm long & 3 mm wide. They sometimes have a single vein visible on the lower surface. There are a few long, soft hairs on the upper surface and edges of the leaves.

The flowers are pink/purple and are borne usually in pairs on the ends of the branches.

They have 5 sepals which are often hairy on the outside surface and 5 petals. The stamens, which give the flower its colour, are arranged in 5 bundles, each containing 14 to 33 stamens. Flowering occurs from December to January and is followed by fruits, which are woody capsules.

Taxonomy and naming

Eremaea purpurea was first formally described in 1964 by Charles Gardner in Journal of the Royal Society of Western Australia. The specific epithet (*purpurea*) is from the Latin *purpureus* meaning "purple".

Distribution and habitat

Eremaea purpurea occurs in the Darling district in Jarrah Forest north and south of Perth.

It grows in sandy soils, often on roadsides and in damp depressions.

Eremaea violacea F.Muell. Violet Eremaea

Description

height of about 1.0 meter and *Eremaea violacea* is a spreading to prostrate shrub which grows to a which has its younger branches densely covered with fine hairs. The leaves are linear to narrow egg-shaped, up to 12 mm long & 1.2 mm wide. They are flat or circular in cross section, depending on subspecies. (The two subspecies can be distinguished from each other by their cross section.)

As suggested by its name, the flowers are violet coloured and are on the ends of short, side branches which grew earlier in the previous year. The flowers occur in groups of up to 7. There are 5 sepals which are usually hairy on the outside surface and 5 petals. The stamens are arranged in 5 bundles, each containing 24 to 32 stamens Flowering occurs from September to October and is followed by fruits which are woody capsules. The capsules are cup shaped to almost spherical and are smooth on the outer surface.

Taxonomy and naming

Eremaea violacea was first formally described in 1878 by Ferdinand von Mueller in Fragmenta Phytographiae Australiae. The specific epithet (*violacea*) is from the Latin *violaceus* meaning "having a purple colour

There are two subspecies:

- *Eremaea violacea* F.Muell. subsp. *violacea* has flat leaves and is restricted to areas between Geraldton and Eneabba, north of Perth.
- *Eremaea violacea* subsp. raphiophylla Hnatiuk has long, thin cylindrical leaves and occurs between the Arrowsmith and Hill rivers - Eneabba & Jurien Bay, north of Perth.

Distribution and habitat

Eremaea violacea is found in the Sandplains south of Geraldton. It grows in sand, sandy clay or soils derived from laterite on sandplains, ridges and roadsides.

Eremaea violacea

Eremaea violacea* subsp. *raphiophylla

Eremaea violacea poss. subsp. *violacea*

Kunzea (K. recurva x K. sulphurea)

Kunzea sp. Poss. similis

Kunzea acicularis Toelken & G.F.Craig

Description

Kunzea acicularis is a shrub which grows to a height of up to 2 m with a few erect, irregularly-branched stems which are covered with fine hairs when young. The leaves are egg-shaped with the narrower end towards the base, densely hairy, up to 6 mm long, about 2 mm wide, with a stalk less than 1 mm long.

Generally, there are three to five pink/mauve flowers arranged in groups on the ends of branches. The flowers are surrounded by hairy, narrow triangular bracts and bracteoles about 3 mm long and 1 mm wide. The sepals are about 2 mm long and hairy and the five petals are up to 4 mm long and almost round. The stamens are usually longer than the petals with a 6 or 7 mm long style. Flowering occurs in October and November and is followed by hairy, urn-shaped fruit. It is similar to the southern form of K. preissiana, but differs in height and has broader leaves.

Taxonomy and naming

This species was first formally described in 2007 by Hellmut Toelken and Gil Craig and the description was published in *Nuytsia*. The specific epithet (acicularis) is a Latin word meaning "like a needle" referring to the needle-like bracts.

Distribution and habitat

This kunzea grows in mallee and heath on pale orange clay loam with, Euc. pleurocarpa,

E. tetraptera, Banksia –affin. Dryandra cirsioides, Hakea laurina & Beaufortia schaueri north-east of Ravensthorpe.

Conservation

Kunzea acicularis is classified as 'Threatened Flora' by the Western Australian Government Department of Parks and Wildlife and an interim recovery plan has been prepared

Authors note: *Did not become aware of the location of this species until shortly before I was to depart on my south-east field trip. It took some finding. All nearby 'roads' were gravel or sand. There is only one known location. The Kunzea had almost finished flowering but I was fortunate to obtain a few images.*

Kunzea acuminata Toelken

Description

Kunzea acuminata is a shrub which grows to a height of up to 2 m, with a few spindly branches covered with long silky hairs when young. The leaf stalk is up to 2 mm long and the leaf blade is linear to lance-shaped, to about 7 mm long and about 1 mm wide. The leaves have long, silky hairs along their margins. The flowers are arranged in roughly spherical heads containing eight to fifteen flowers on the ends of the branches which continue to grow after flowering. The flowers are surrounded by silky bracts to about 7 mm and bracteoles about 5 mm long. The five sepals are egg-shaped, up to 1.5 mm and silky-hairy and the five petals are about 2 mm long and pink. There are about fifty stamens up to 4.5 mm long. Flowering occurs in September.

K acuminata is similar to K similis in its sparse though more woody habit, and inflorescences with more flowers.

Taxonomy and naming

This species was first formally described in 1996 by Hellmut Toelken and the description was published in *Journal of the Adelaide Botanic Garden*. The specific epithet (acuminata) is a Latin word meaning "pointed" or "sharpened"

Distribution and habitat

K acuminata is only known from an area east of Israelite Bay where it grows in sandy soil.

Conservation

Kunzea acuminata is classified as "not threatened" by the Western Australian Government Department of Parks and Wildlife.

Authors Note:

Unfortunately, I was unable to visit the Israelite Bay location during my SE Field trip, nor was an example of K. acuminata available to look at in the West Australian Herbarium at the time.

The image was found on website: earth.com.

Kunzea affinis S.Moore

Description

Kunzea affinis is a shrub which grows to a height of up to 1.5 m and a width of about 1 m. It usually has a few erect branches terminating in many intricate, short side branches and which are hairy when young. The leaf stalk is less than 1 mm long and the leaf blade is linear, 4–6 mm long and less than 1 mm wide. The leaves are erect or pressed against the stem and have long hairs, mainly along their margins.

The flowers are arranged in groups of two to five, on the ends of the branches which continue to grow after flowering. The flowers are surrounded by woolly bracts and bracteoles about 1.5 mm long. The five sepals are broad egg-shaped and glabrous. The five petals are oval to spoon-shaped, and rose-pink. There are about 20 to 25 rose-pink stamens with bright yellow anthers. Flowering occurs from August to October and is followed by fruit which look like small capsules releasing many small seeds when ripe.

Taxonomy and naming

Kunzea affinis was first formally described in 1920 by Spencer Moore and the description was published in *Journal of the Adelaide Botanic Garden*. The specific epithet (affinis) is Latin, meaning "related to". (Moore noted the similarity of this species to *Kunzea pauciflora*.

Known Hybrids:

K. affinis x K. jucunda – Leaves are not linear and bracts are more rounded. **(Refer bottom photo)**

K. affinis x K. preissiana – Quite common. Different to K. preissiana by the appressed hairs on the lower leaf surfaces.

Distribution and habitat

This Kunzea grows in sandy soils in a range of habitats including kwongan, in scrubby vegetation and along rivers, mainly between Ravensthorpe and Esperance.

Use in horticulture

This Kunzea has been in cultivation for many years. It can be most easily propagated from cuttings collected in spring or early summer or from seed but the seed is difficult to collect. It does best in areas where rainfall is mostly in winter and in well drained soils. K. affinis will tolerate some shade and at least moderate frost and can be kept in shaped by light tip pruning.

Kunzea ambigua (Sm.) Druce

Poverty Bush or Tick Bush

Description

Kunzea ambigua is a small- to medium-sized spreading shrub that may reach 5m both in height and width, though is usually much smaller (from 1m). Its bark is fibrous and furrowed, while the narrow lanceolate green leaves are 0.5–1.3cm in length and 0.2cm wide, with hairy new growth. Occurring from September to December or January, the white flowers are 1.2cm in diameter and sweetly fragrant. The stamens are longer than the petals. The flowers are followed by small woody capsules 0.4cm in diameter.

Taxonomy and naming

Kunzea ambigua was first formally described in 1797 by James Edward Smith who gave it the name *Leptospermum ambiguum*. English botanist George Claridge Druce gave it its current name in 1917. The generic name honours German naturalist Gustav Kunze, while the specific epithet is derived from the Latin adjective *ambiguus* meaning "doubtful" or "uncertain".

A pink-flowered hybrid - possibly with *Kunzea capitata* - has been recorded from Stony Range Flora reserve in Dee Why in Sydney's northern beaches region.

Distribution and habitat

Kunzea ambigua is found from northeastern New South Wales, having been recorded in the Grand High Tops of the Warrumbungle National Park, through Victoria and into Tasmania. It grows on sandy soils in coastal or near-coastal regions. It is a very common dry forest shrub of the Sydney region, and regenerates in disturbed or cleared areas.

In recent times, *Kunzea ambigua* has been introduced to Flinders Island and North East Tasmania. It grows abundantly in both locations Tasmania regularly experiences strong westerly winds and a high annual rainfall of over 700mm. This harsh, windy and brisk climate is an ideal environment for *K.ambigua* to thrive. In particular, this wind has played a key role in blanketing Flinders Island and many parts of Tasmania with Kunzea seed and thus it grows profusely throughout the island.

Use in horticulture

It was one of the first species of Australian plant introduced into cultivation in England. It is a hardy and adaptable plant that is used in windbreaks and sand dune stabilization plantings, as well as gardens, particularly in Australian gardens using native plants according to principles of natural landscaping. The species attracts Australian native insects, and can provide shelter for small birds and the long-nosed bandicoot. It can regenerate quickly after disturbance.

Authors Note: *I have grown the pink hybrid successfully in Perth's sandy soils.*

Photo: Wikimedia commons

Kunzea baxteri (Klotzsch) Schauer

Description

Kunzea baxteri is a spreading shrub which usually grows to a height of between 1m and 3m and has branches which are more or less hairy. The leaves are arranged alternately on a petiole 1–2mm long and have a leaf blade that is usually 14–18mm long, 2.5–3.5mm wide and oblong to elliptic in shape with hairs along the edges.

The flowers are arranged in large, profuse, conspicuous, bottlebrush-like clusters, up to 10cm long and 6cm wide. The clusters usually contain between 16 and 30 flowers on the ends of branches which continue to grow during the flowering period. There are leaf-like bracts 5–9mm long, 2–3mm wide at the base of the flowers which fall off as the flowers open. The hypanthium is 7–9mm long and hairy on the outside. There are five hairy, linear to lance-shaped sepals 4.5–6mm long which remain on the maturing fruit. There are between 40 and 50 bright red stamens 19–24mm long around each flower, the stamens four or five times as long as the petals. Flowering is most prolific from July to September but often occurs as late as March, depending on rainfall. The fruit is a cup-shaped or urn-shaped capsule 8–10mm long with the erect sepals attached. The fruit release the seeds when mature, unlike many others in the Myrtaceae. The features of this species that distinguish it from others in the Myrtaceae are the red flowers, persistent sepals and deciduous fruit. The oblong leaves and narrow sepals distinguish it from *K. pulchella* which also has red flowers

Taxonomy and naming

The species was first formally described in 1836 by Johann Klotzsch, who gave it the name *Pentagonaster baxteri* and published the description in *Allgemeine Gartenzeitung*. In 1844, Johannes Conrad Schauer revised the name to *Kunzea baxteri*. The specific epithet (baxteri) honours William Baxter, an English gardener who collected seeds and plants for British nurserymen

Distribution and habitat

Kunzea baxteri grows in coarse sandy soil or laterite, often near granite outcrops in heath, scrub or woodland. It is found in coastal areas of Western Australia, roughly between Esperance and Israelite Bay.

Use in horticulture

This kunzea has been grown in gardens for many years. It is best suited to a climate with dry summers and wet winters. It is, however, adaptable to more humid areas and those with moderate frosts but requires a sunny or partly-shaded area with well-drained soil. In has been grown from cuttings on *Kunzea ambigua* rootstock.

Kunzea cambagei Maiden & Betche

Description

Kunzea cambagei is a shrub which grows to a height of about 0.6 m with its branches silky-hairy when young. The leaves are arranged alternately along the branches, elliptic to egg-shaped with the narrower end towards the base, up to 8 mm long and 3 mm wide with a petiole about 0.5 mm long. The flowers are cream-colored to yellowish and arranged in rounded groups of five to twelve near the ends of the branches. The floral cup is silky-hairy and about 3 mm long. The sepal lobes are triangular, about 1 mm long and the petals are white, about 2 mm long. There are approximately 20-25 stamens which are 2 or 3 mm long. Flowering occurs in October and November and the fruit are cup-shaped capsules.

Taxonomy and naming

K. cambagei was first formally described in 1913 by Joseph Maiden and Ernst Betche from a specimen collected by Richard Hind Cambage. The description was published in *Proceedings of the Linnean Society of New South Wales*. The specific epithet (*cambagei*) honors the collector of the type specimen.

Distribution and habitat

Kunzea cambagei grows in moist heath, mainly on the Central Tablelands of New South Wales.

Conservation

K. cambagei is listed as "Vulnerable" under the Commonwealth Government *Environment Protection and Biodiversity Conservation Act 1999* (EPBC) Act and as "Vulnerable" under the New South Wales *Threatened Species Conservation Act 1995*. The main threats to the species are inappropriate fire regimes and habitat degradation caused by road widening, rubbish dumping and trail bikes.

(Photo: Wikimedia commons – unknown photographer)

Kunzea capitata (Sm.) Heynh.

Description

The species has a spreading or erect habit and may grow up to 2 meters in height. Flowers are pink to purple, or occasionally white. These are produced on the branch ends in "heads". Leaves are 3.5–9 millimeters long and 1.5–4.5 millimetres wide, with recurved tips and 1 mm long petioles.

Taxonomy

The species was first formally described by English botanist James Smith in 1797 in *Transactions of the Linnean Society of London*, and given the name *Metrosideros capitata*. The species epithet *capitata* is derived from the Latin word *caput* (head), alluding to the arrangement of the flowers.

It was transferred to the genus *Kunzea* in 1846 by German botanist Gustav Heynhold.

Distribution and habitat

The species occurs in heathland and dry sclerophyll forest from the Ulladulla district northward to Richmond River in New South Wales.

Cultivation

The species prefers a moist soil in a lightly shaded to sunny position.

It is readily propagated by either seed or cuttings.

Kunzea poss. ciliata Toelken

Description

Kunzea ciliata is a spreading shrub which usually grows to a height of 0.8–1.5mm with its branches densely hairy when young but glabrous later when corky bark develops. The leaves are narrow elliptic to lance-shaped with the narrower end towards the base, mostly 4–5mm long and about 1.5mm wide with a petiole up to 0.5mm long. The flowers are pink or pale pink and arranged in rounded clusters of twelve to eighteen mostly near the ends of longer branches which continue to grow after flowering. There are more or less hairy, leaf-like bracts 2–3mm long and smaller bracteoles in pairs at the base of the flowers. There are approximately 45 stamens in several rows, each stamen 3.5–5mm long. Flowering occurs in October and November but sometimes in other months when conditions are favorable. The fruit that follows flowering is an urn-shaped capsule with the remains of the sepals attached.

Taxonomy and naming

Kunzea ciliata was first formally described in 1996 by Hellmut Toelken and the description was published in *Journal of the Adelaide Botanic Garden*. The specific epithet (ciliata) is derived from the Latin word *cilium* meaning "eyelash", referring to the hairy bracts

Distribution and habitat

Often found on or among granite slopes and gneiss outcrops in coastal areas. *K. ciliata* occurs between Cape Naturaliste and Cape Leeuwin where it grows in loamy sand soils.

Kunzea cincinnata Toelken

Description

Kunzea cincinnata is a shrub with a few main stems and many shorter branches and which grows to a height of 1 m. The leaves are linear to lance-shaped with the narrow end towards the base and up to 7mm long and less than 1 mm wide. The flowers are arranged in groups of up to three on the ends of the shorter branches. They are surrounded by hairy bracts 3–5 mm long and shorter pairs of bracteoles. The floral cup is about 3 mm and the five sepals are egg-shaped and hairy and about 1 mm long. The five petals are about 3 mm long and pink to deep magenta. There are about thirty stamens which are slightly longer than the petals. Flowering occurs in September and October and is followed by urn-shaped fruit.

Taxonomy and naming

Kunzea cincinnata was first formally described in 1996 by Hellmut R. Toelken from a specimen collected near Ravensthorpe and the description was published in *Journal of the Adelaide Botanic Gardens*. The specific epithet (*cincinnata*) is a Latin word meaning "curly", referring to the hairs on the branches and leaves, distinguishing this species from the similar *K. affinis*.

Hybrid: K. cincinnata x K jucunda: Leaves are more or less elliptic and glabrous. Young branches and leaves are covered with coiled hairs and the bracts gradually taper to a point (acuminate) as in K cincinnata.

Distribution and habitat

This Kunzea is often found between Ravensthorpe and Esperance south-east of Perth growing in gravelly loam soils over laterite.

Kunzea clavata Toelken

Description

Kunzea clavata is a shrub or tree with several main stems and many branches and which grows to a height of 2.5–4 m. The leaves are linear, lance-shaped or shaped like a baseball bat, 3 or 4 mm long and less than 1 mm wide with a petiole less than 1 mm long. The flowers are arranged in dense heads mainly on the ends of the longer branches. The flowers are surrounded by generally glabrous bracts and shorter pairs of bracteoles. The floral cup is about 3 mm long and the five sepals are triangular, glabrous and about 1 mm long. The five petals are about 2 mm long and pale yellow and there 30-35 stamens. Flowering occurs in September and October and is followed by urn shaped fruit.

Taxonomy and naming

Kunzea clavata was first formally described in 1996 by Hellmut R. Toelken from a specimen collected near Bornholm and the description was published in *Journal of the Adelaide Botanic Gardens*. The specific epithet (*clavata*) is derived from the Latin word "clava", meaning 'club', referring to the leaves often being shaped like a baseball bat.

Distribution and habitat

K. clavata is found around lakes and marshy areas near Walpole and Denmark in the south of Western Australia, but it is very restricted in its distribution.

Authors note: *Had one confirmed location for this Kunzea near Walpole, but I found only one specimen at the nominated location. It was raining and cold when I came across it; and I had to dash out of the car in between the showers to obtain some images. You can see the rainwater glistening on the photos.*

Kunzea ericifolia (Sm.) Heynh. Spearwood

Description

Kunzea ericifolia is a woody erect shrub, often multi-stemmed, that can grow to a height of 6 meters. The long and slender stems divide from the base, and continue to divide into finer, flexible and narrowly angled branches. The shrub has a crown of soft pale green foliage. The leaf are simple in structure with linear form growing to a length of about 10 mm with a width of 1 mm. Flowering occurs in spring (July to December) and produces small round flowers approximately 10 mm in diameter. The globular blossom is perfumed and yellow, cream or white in color and occurs in clusters and the ends of branches. Flowers are followed by small single celled fruits that contain many small seed that are dispersed once the fruit is ripe. The bark is fibrous, rough and grey in colour, often peeling in layers from the stem.

Taxonomy and naming

K. ericifolia was first formally described in 1812 by James Edward Smith who gave it the name *Metrosideros ericifolia* from a specimen collected by Archibald Menzies during the Vancouver expedition's stop at King George Sound in 1791. The description was published in *The Cyclopedia* edited by Abraham Rees. When he published his description of the genus *Kunzea* in 1828, Ludwig Reichenbach referred to *Kunzea ericifolia* but did not validly publish the name. However, in 1840 Gustav Heynhold published the name in *Alphabetische und Synonymische Aufzahlung der in den Jahren 1840 bis 1846 in den europäischen Gärten eingeführten Gewächse nebst Angabe ihres Autors*. The specific epithet (*ericifolia*) is a reference to the apparent similarity of the leaves of this species to those of *Erica* in the family Ericaceae.

Distribution

Kunzea ericifolia is widespread in Southwest Australia. Populations are found as far north as Gingin and as far east as Bremer Bay on the south coast. The largest populations occur around Albany. Many communities are found along the coast-line. A southeastern population is found in the Fitzgerald River National Park. Stands are often found in transition areas between wetlands and drier regions.

The name of a Perth W.A. Suburb – Spearwood - is reputed to have been the common name for Kunzea *ericifolia*. The first time the name was used was when the Developer, James Morrison sub-divided the area in 1897 creating the 'Spearwood Garden Estate.

Use in horticulture

The plant has been cultivated for many years as an ornamental plant. It is easily propagated by seed or by cutting and considered to have greater potential as a garden plant than is currently recognised.

Kunzea eriocalyx F.Muell.

Description

Kunzea eriocalyx is a shrub with spreading stems with a few short branches and which grows to a height of 1m–1.5m. The leaves are mostly clustered on the ends of the side branches which also have groups of flowers in the flowering season. The leaves are linear, more or less shaped like a baseball bat, 2.5–4.5mm long and less than 1mm wide with a petiole up to 1mm long. The flowers are arranged in heads of mostly five to seven on the ends of the side branches. The pink flowers are surrounded by hairy bracts 3mm long and 2mm wide and shorter pairs of bracteoles. There are eleven to fifteen stamens. Flowering occurs between August and October and is followed by fruit which are urn-shaped capsules with the sepals attached.

Taxonomy and naming

Kunzea eriocalyx was first formally described in 1860 by the botanist Ferdinand von Mueller and the description was published in the work *Fragmenta Phytographiae Australiae*. The type specimen was collected in the Middle Mount Barren. The specific epithet (*eriocalyx*) is derived from the Greek words *erion* meaning "wool" and *kalyx* meaning "cup"...

Distribution and habitat

Often found among rocky outcrops of quartzite, *K. eriocalyx* grows in a small area within the Fitzgerald River National Park where it grows in sandy clay soils of laterite.

Conservation

Kunzea eriocalyx is classified as "Priority Two" by the Western Australian Government Department of Parks and Wildlife meaning that it is poorly known and from very few locations.

Authors Note: *I found this Kunzea one of the most difficult to locate. I travelled through the western side of the Fitzgerald River National Park; entering from Bremer Bay and exiting near Jerramungup; on mostly gravel roads. There was lots to see and the gravel was quite well graded, but K eriocalyx was very difficult to pick up. The GPS co-ordinates were helpful but not precise, so I had to do what I usually do on these trips – drive extremely slowly all the way along the road, stopping regularly when I spotted something of interest.*

I have not been able to find any photos of Kunzea eriocalyx anywhere, with which to compare my photos. I have included an image of a dried & mounted specimen of this plant from the Western Australian Herbarium.

Kunzea glabrescens Toelken

Description

Kunzea glabrescens is a shrub or tree with several main stems and many branches and which grows to a height of up to 4m. The leaves are linear to lance-shaped with the narrower end towards the base, mostly 5–8mm long and less than 1mm wide with a petiole up to 1mm long. The flowers are white-pale yellow in colour and arranged in dense heads of 18 to 28 mainly on the ends of the longer branches. The flowers are surrounded by egg-shaped bracts 2–3mm long and 1–2.5 mm wide and pairs of broadly egg-shaped bracteoles which are 2mm long and 3mm wide. Stamens number 30-45. Flowering mostly occurs in October and November and is followed by fruit which are urn-shaped capsules.

Taxonomy and naming

Kunzea glabrescens was first formally described in 1996 by Hellmut R. Toelken from a specimen collected near Lake Goolelal in Greenwood and the description was published in *Journal of the Adelaide Botanic Gardens*. The specific epithet (*glabrescens*) is derived from the Latin word *glaber* meaning "hairless", "bald" or "smooth" and the suffix *-escens* meaning "becoming", referring to the leaves being hairless or becoming so with age. The genus was named after Gustav Kunze who was a professor of botany, entomologist and physician

Distribution and habitat

Kunzea glabrescens typically grows in sandy soil and is often found in wet depressions and along watercourses as far north as Gingin and then south through the Swan Coastal Plain, Peel Region through the South West region extending into the Great Southern region as far east as Albany.

Kunzea jucunda Diels & E.Pritz.

Description

Kunzea jucunda is a shrub with a few erect main stems and many short side branches. It usually grows to a height of 0.6–1.2 m and is mostly glabrous except for a few hairs around the flowers and youngest leaves. The leaves are glabrous, mostly elliptic in shape, about 3 mm long and about 2 mm wide with a petiole less than 1 mm long. The flowers are arranged in heads of mostly two to four on the ends of the side branches. The flowers are surrounded by bracts which are mostly glabrous except for a few hairs around the edges and by pairs of smaller bracteoles. The floral cup is about 3 mm long and the five sepals are lance-shaped and glabrous. The five petals are spatula-shaped to almost round, about and pink to deep mauve. There are 18-24 stamens in several rows in each flower. Flowering occurs mainly between August and October and is followed by fruit which are urn-shaped with five vertical ridges. K.jucunda is similar to *K. affinis* but is distinguished mainly by the mostly glabrous leaves and bracts. However, where the ranges of the two species meet, hybrids often occur.

Taxonomy and naming

Kunzea jucunda was first formally described in 1904 by Ludwig Diels and Ernst Georg Pritzel and the description was published in the journal *Botanische Jahrbucher fur Systematik, Pflanzengeschichte und Pflanzengeographie*. The specific epithet (*jucunda*) is a Latin word meaning "pleasant or delightful".

Varieties: K.jucunda x K.preissiana – difference to K.preissiana: very broad, lower bracts.

K.cincinnata x K.jucunda – young branches and leaves are covered with coiled hairs.

K.affinis x K.jucunda – the leaves are not linear, but distinctly concave above.

Distribution and habitat

This Kunzea grows in a wide range of habitats, but often occurs on sandy or rocky soils of undulating plains, South West of Ravensthorpe.

Kunzea micrantha Schauer

Description

Kunzea micrantha is an erect shrub which typically grows to a height of 0.3 to 1.5 metres usually with many mains stems with a moderate number of thin, wiry side branches. The leaves are linear to lance-shaped with the narrower end towards the base, about 1–7mm long and 0.5-2mm wide with a petiole less than 1mm long. The flowers are pink-purple to white-cream and arranged in heads of mostly twenty to forty on the ends of long stems. The flowers are surrounded by bracts which are 1.5–3mm long and about 1mm wide, mostly glabrous except for a few hairs around the edges and by pairs of smaller bracteoles. There are 12 to 40 stamens 2.5–3.5mm long in several rows in each flower. Flowering occurs mainly between September and December and is followed by fruit which are urn-shaped capsules with the sepals remaining. This kunzea is similar to *K. affinis* but is distinguished mainly by the mostly glabrous leaves and bracts.

It is similar to *Kunzea micromera* and *K. praestans*, sometimes forming hybrids with those species and is difficult to distinguish from them where the ranges overlap.

Taxonomy and naming

Kunzea micrantha was first formally described in 1844 by the botanist Johannes Conrad Schauer in Johann Georg Christian Lehmann's work *Plantae Preissianae*

There are four subspecies of this kunzea:

- *Kunzea micrantha* subsp. *micrantha* which grows in a few swamps on the Swan Coastal Plain from Perth to Busselton with scattered populations near Augusta.
- *Kunzea micrantha* subsp. *petiolata* which grows in temporary swamps on the coastal plain from near the Swan River to near Jurien Bay.
- *Kunzea micrantha* subsp. *oligandra* which is mostly found inland from near Manjimup to Porongorup and also near Bremer Bay, growing in temporary marshes.
- *Kunzea micrantha* subsp. h*irtiflora* which is only known from two locations near Lake Muir where it grows in temporary marshes.

Distribution and habitat

Often found in wet depressions and marshes in coastal areas in the Jarrah Forest, Mallee and Swan Coastal Plain – generally from Pinjarra to Augusta.

Kunzea micrantha grows in sandy, clay and loamy soils.

Fruit

Kunzea micromera Schauer

Description

Kunzea micromera is sparsely branched shrub which typically grows to a height of 30 to 90cm usually with a few main stems each with a few side branches. The leaves are elliptic to lance-shaped with the narrower end towards the base, mostly 1.5–3mm long and about 1mm wide with a petiole less than 0.5mm long. The flower colour is pink and they are arranged in heads of mostly on the ends of a few long shoots. The flowers are surrounded by egg-shaped bracts which are 2–3mm long and 1.5–2.5mm wide and mostly glabrous and by pairs of slightly smaller bracteoles. Flowering occurs between August and November and is followed by fruit which are urn-shaped capsules.

Taxonomy and naming

Kunzea micromera was first formally described in 1848 by the botanist Johannes Conrad Schauer in Johann Georg Christian Lehmann's work *Plantae Preissianae*. The specific epithet (*micromera*) is derived from the Greek words *mikros* meaning "small" and *meros* meaning "part".

Even though K micromera and its variations has been recorded from many areas it is considered relatively rare, as it is not common in these areas.

Variations include: K. micromera x K. montana – larger inflorescences.

K. micromera x K preissiana – all parts of the variety are initially very hairy but becoming glabrous with age.

K. micromera x K. recurva: rigid branches and many inflorescences – **refer image**

Distribution and habitat

Often found in wet depressions and the margins of swamps between Narrogin, Manjimup and Ravensthorpe. *K. micromera* grows in sandy or clay soils.

Kunzea micromera x K. recurva

Kunzea montana (Diels) Domin Mountain Kunzea

Description

Kunzea montana is a shrub, sometimes a small tree growing to a height of 2 m, with rigid branches. The leaves are glabrous, egg-shaped to almost circular, up to 5 mm long and wide, not including the petiole which is another 2 mm long.

The flowers are arranged in spherical groups of 18 to 32, on the ends of branches which continue to grow after flowering. The flowers are cream-coloured to pale yellow and are surrounded by glabrous, egg-shaped bracts and bracteoles. The floral cup and sepals are each about 1 mm long and the five petals are egg-shaped to almost round and about 3 mm long. There are about 50 to 70 stamens which are about twice as long as the petals and a style about 7 mm long. Flowering occurs in October and November and is followed by fruit which are urn-shaped.

Taxonomy and naming

This species was first formally described in 1904 by Ludwig Diels as a variety of *Kunzea recurva* and the description was published in *Botanische Jahrbucher fur Systematik, Pflanzengeschichte und Pflanzengeographie*. In 1923, Karel Domin raised it to species status, publishing the change in *Vestnik Kralovske Ceske Spolecnosti Nauk, Trida Matematiko-Prirodevedecke*. The specific epithet (montana) is a Latin word meaning "of mountains".

A pink flowering hybrid of *K montana* referred to as *K.montana* x *K. recurva* is illustrated.

Distribution and habitat

K.montana primarily grows on the rocky slopes in the Stirling Range National Park south of Perth.

Kunzea muelleri Benth.

Description

Kunzea muelleri is a low, spreading shrub which grows to a height up to less than 1 m with its branches sometimes forming random (adventitious) roots. The leaves are arranged in more or less opposite pairs and are linear, more or less cylindrical in shape, up to about 5 mm long and less than 1 mm wide with an almost non-existent petiole. The flowers are arranged in groups of mostly two or three near the ends of the branches. The bracts are egg-shaped to about 4 mm long and 2 mm wide and the bracteoles at the base of the flowers are about the same size. The floral cup is hairy and up to about 4 mm long. The sepals are egg-shaped to triangular, about 2 mm long and hairy. The petals are pale yellow, more or less round and about 2 mm long. There are about 24-35 stamens which can be up to 5 mm long. Flowering occurs from November to January and is followed by fleshy fruit with thin skin and a central stone containing the seed.

Taxonomy and naming

Kunzea muelleri was first formally described in 1867 English botanist George Bentham in his publication *Flora Australiensis* from a specimen collected by Victorian Government Botanist Ferdinand von Mueller. Mueller collected plants from the Haidinger Range, Mount Wellington and the Munyang Mountains and had given the species the name *Kunzea ericifolia* in 1855. This name was later changed as it had already been assigned to another species. The specific epithet (*muelleri*) honours Mueller.

Distribution and habitat

This Kunzea grows in alpine, subalpine and montane heath and is common in rocky areas. It sometimes forms extensive stands. In the Kosciuszko National Park in New South Wales, groups of plants up to only 20 cm high cover large areas.

(Photo: Wikimedia commons – Author is referred to as 'Melburnian')

Kunzea newbeyi Toelken

Description

Kunzea newbeyi is a robust shrub with several main stems and many side branches and which grows to a height of 0.6–2.3 m. The leaves are glabrous, oblong to lance-shaped with the narrower end towards the base, up to 6mm long and about 2 mm wide, not including the petiole which is about an additional 2 mm long. The flowers are arranged in more or less spherical groups of 15 to 35, on the ends of branches which continue to grow after flowering. They are surrounded by glabrous, egg-shaped bracts and bracteoles. The floral cup is glabrous and the five sepals are egg-shaped. The five petals are mid to deep pink, egg-shaped and there are about 40 to 50 stamens which are about twice as long as the petals. The style is up to 8 mm long. Flowering occurs in October and November and is followed by urn-shaped fruit.

Taxonomy and naming

Kunzea newbeyi was first formally described by Hellmut R. Toelken in 1996 in the article

A revision of the genus Kunzea (Myrtaceae) in the *Journal of the Adelaide Botanic Garden*. The specific epithet (*newbeyi*) honours Mr. K. Newbey, who was the first to make a collection of this species.

Distribution and habitat

This Kunzea is found on the dry lower slopes of breakaway areas in a small area along the southern coast of Western Australia.

Conservation

Kunzea newbeyi is found in very few locations, however it has recently been discovered in numbers, west of Bremer Bay, near Corackerup Nature Reserve. It is classified by the Government of Western Australia, Department of Parks and Wildlife as "Priority One." This means that is only known from a few locations, which are potentially at risk.

Authors Note: *I visited all known locations for K. newbeyi but was only successful at finding the plant in the above location. I almost missed it because it was in the latter stages of flowering; the remaining flowers having faded, and the foliage colour blending into the surrounding vegetation.*

Kunzea obovata Byrnes

Description

Kunzea obovata is an erect, spreading shrub which grows to a height of up to 3 m with its branches silky hairy when young. The leaves are egg-shaped with the narrower end towards the base, have a dished upper surface and a down-turned tip. They are up to 9 mm long and about 1 mm wide with a very small petiole and are covered with soft hairs when young. The flowers are arranged in clusters of up to eighteen or more flowers on the ends of the branches. The floral cup is about 3 mm long and hairy. The sepals are broadly triangular, about 1 mm long and pointed. The petals are deep purplish, sometimes pink, egg-shaped, about 2 mm long and there 35 to 50 stamens which are up to 5 mm long. The style is about 5 mm long. Flowering occurs mostly from September to November and the fruit are urn-shaped capsules.

Taxonomy and naming

Kunzea obovata was first formally described in 1982 by Norman Byrnes and the description was published in *Journal of the Adelaide Botanic Garden*. The specific epithet (obovata) is a Latin word meaning "egg-shaped".

Distribution and habitat

This Kunzea is restricted to northern New South Wales and south-eastern Queensland.

It grows in forest in soils derived from granite, on the tablelands north from Deepwater. It is found in Girraween and Boonoo National Parks.

(Image: Wikimedia commons)

Kunzea opposita
F.Muell.

Description

Kunzea opposita is a spindly shrub which grows to a height of 0.5–3 m with its young stems covered with fine hairs. The leaves are mostly arranged in opposite pairs along the branches and are narrow egg-shaped, 1–3 mm long and less than 1 mm wide on a very short petiole. The leaves are glabrous. The flowers are arranged in rounded groups of five to nine on the ends of the branches. There are lance-shaped to egg-shaped bracts which are 2–3 mm long and 1–2 mm wide, and smaller paired bracteoles at the base the flowers. The floral cup is 3–4 mm long and hairy. The sepals are triangular to egg-shaped, 1–1.5 mm long and sometimes hairy. The petals are pink, oblong to broadly egg-shaped, about 1.5 mm long and there are 40 to 50 stamens in several rows. The stamens are 3–5 mm long. Flowering occurs in August to November and is followed by fruit which an urn-shaped capsule about 3 mm long and wide with the sepal lobes attached.

Taxonomy and naming

Kunzea opposita was first formally described in 1867 by Ferdinand von Mueller and the description was published in *Fragmenta phytographiae Australiae*. The specific epithet (*opposita*) is a Latin word meaning "on the other side" or "contrary".

Distribution and habitat

This Kunzea grows in woodland, forest or exposed cliffs north of the Mount Kaputar National Park and in south-east Queensland.

(Image: Wikimedia commons)

Kunzea parvifolia Schauer

Description

Kunzea parvifolia is a wiry shrub which usually grows to a height of 0.5–1.5m with its young branches covered with soft hairs. The leaves are linear to narrow lance-shaped and more or less pressed against the stem. They are 1–4mm long, about 1mm wide with a petiole less than 1mm long and are covered with soft hairs when young. The flowers are arranged in clusters of mostly three to eight on the ends of the branches. The petals are pink to mauve, occasionally white, egg-shaped to almost round, about 2mm long and there 30 to 40 stamens which are 2–3.5mm long.

The style is 2.5–3.5mm long. Flowering mostly occurs in October and November and the fruit are urn-shaped capsules which are about 2mm long and wide.

Taxonomy and naming

Kunzea parvifolia was first formally described in 1844 by Johannes Conrad Schauer and the description was published in Johann Lehmann's *Plantae Preissianae*. The specific epithet (*parvifolia*) is derived from the Latin words *parvus* meaning "small" and *folium* meaning "leaf"

Distribution and habitat

This kunzea grows in forest in heath and forest in eastern New South Wales south from Torrington and in Victoria, mainly in the north-east but with isolated locations further west.

Use in horticulture

K. parvifolia has been available for cultivation for a number of years, and is readily grown from seed or cutting. It prefers a well-drained, sunny position.

(Image: Wikimedia commons)

Kunzea pauciflora Schauer

Description
The erect and compact shrub typically grows to a height of 0.35 to 1.5 metres. It blooms between August and November producing pink flowers.

Taxonomy and naming
The species was first formally described by the botanist Johannes Conrad Schauer in 1844 in Johann Georg Christian Lehmann's work *Plantae Preissianae*. The name of the plant is often misapplied to *Kunzea affinis*. The specific epithet *pauciflora*, refers to the Latin term for 'few flowered'

Distribution and habitat
Found on hillside and slopes in coastal areas of the Great Southern regions of Western Australia in a small area east of Albany centered in the Fitzgerald River National Park where it grows in gravelly sandy or loamy soils over limestone or sandstone.

Conservation
Kunzea pauciflora was classified in 1995, as "Priority Four" by the West Australian Government Department of Parks and Wildlife. This meant that in 1995 K. Pauciflora was considered rare & endangered.

Kunzea pomifera F. Muell. 'Muntries'

Description

Best described as a ground cover, capable of covering an area of 5m or 6m, but not much more than 0.5m high. Leaves are bright green, relatively stiff, petiolate and rounded with recurved margins – about 5mm long. Generally white flowers from September to December - glabrous calyx tubes. Fruit are about 1cm in diameter, green with a reddish hue at maturity, and apparently edible.

Taxonomy and naming

Kunzea pomifera was first described in 1855 by F.J.H. von Mueller in a publication - *Definitions of rare or hitherto undescribed Australian plants*.

Distribution and habitat

K. pomifera is a low-growing shrub, found along the southern coast of Australia - predominantly South Australia and Victoria

Trellising

While K. pomifera are a groundcover in the wild, commercial growers have successfully managed to trellis the plants. Trellised 'Muntries' allow easier access for harvesting and management. It also allows a more efficient use of orchard space.

K. pomifera can be trained quite easily through weaving the growing plant through and along trellis wires, using plant ties to secure them.

Cultivation

K. pomifera was grown in England in 1889. It was one of the first species of Australian plant introduced into cultivation in England.

The plant prefers a well-drained soil of a moderately acid to strongly alkaline pH. For cultivation it is suggested that waterlogging and extremely dry soils should both be avoided. Moderate restriction of water in the early spring may be beneficial in stimulating flowering and reducing competitive vegetative growth.

Kunzea praestans Schauer

Description & Distribution

This erect shrub typically grows to a height of 0.3 to 2 metres. It blooms between September and October producing pink-purple flowers.

Often found on hillslopes of the Wheatbelt region of Western Australia south-east of Perth generally between Wickepin and Kulin, where it grows in lateritic soils.

Taxonomy and naming

The species was first formally described by the botanist Johannes Conrad Schauer in 1844 in Johann Georg Christian Lehmann's work *Plantae Preissianae*. There are two synonyms for the species; *Kunzea recurva* var. *praestans* and *Kunzea incognita*.

Kunzea preissiana Schauer

Description & Distribution

This erect shrub typically grows to a height of 0.5 to 1.8 metres. Leaves are small, about 5mm long; oblanceolate and glabrous. The numerous pink flowers are mostly seen in clusters at the ends of the branches; blooming between August and October.

Often found in the southern Goldfields-Esperance regions –generally between Ravensthorpe and the Fitzgerald River National Park of Western Australia, where it grows in sandy and gravelly lateritic soils.

Taxonomy and naming

The species was first formally described by the botanist Johannes Conrad Schauer in 1844 in Johann Georg Christian Lehmann's work *Plantae Preissianae*.

Hybrids for the species:

Kunzea affinis x K. preissiana

Kunzea jucunda x K. preissiana

Kunzea micromera x K. preissiana

Kunzea pulchella (Lindl.) A.S.George Granite Kunzea

Description

Kunzea pulchella is a spreading shrub which usually grows to a height of between 0.6 and 3m often with few side-branches, the branches more or less hairy. The leaves are arranged alternately on a petiole up to 1 mm long and have a leaf blade that is usually 5–14mm long, 2.5–5.5mm wide and egg-shaped to lance-shaped with the narrower end towards the base. Both sides of the leaves are silky-hairy.

The flowers are arranged in loose groups of 6 to 14, each flower on a stalk 2.5–4.5mm long on the ends of branches which often continue to grow during the flowering period. There are leaf-like, egg-shaped bracts 4.5–6mm long and smaller bracteoles at the base of the flower and which fall off as the flower develops. The hypanthium is 4–5mm long and densely hairy on the outside. There are five hairy, pointed, triangular sepals 2–3.5mm long, which remain on the maturing fruit. The five petals are deep red, almost round and 3.5–5mm long. There are more than 70 bright red stamens 10–17mm long around each flower, the stamens are three or four times as long as the petals.

Some forms of the plant have white to pale cream-coloured flowers. Flowering generally occurs from June to November and is followed by fruit which is in the form of a broad, urn-shaped capsule 4–5mm long with the erect sepals attached

Taxonomy and naming

The species was first formally described in 1839 by John Lindley, who gave it the name *Salisia pulchella* and published the description in *A Sketch of the Vegetation of the Swan River Colony*.

In 1966, Alex George revised the name to *Kunzea pulchella* and published the change in *The Western Australian Naturalist*. The specific epithet (pulchella) is the diminutive of the Latin word *pulcher* meaning "pretty", hence "beautiful little"

Distribution and habitat

K. pulchella grows in sandy or clay soils, often near granite outcrops in open scrub.

It generally grows east of Perth, over a widespread area from Kelleberrin to Coolgardie.

Use in horticulture

K.pulchella is an outstanding, ornamental shrub, quite long-lived; requiring a well-drained, sunny position. It is best suited to a climate with dry summers and wet winters but can be grown in Eastern Australian states, if grown from cuttings of. Kunzea ambigua rootstock.

Kunzea recurva Schauer

Description & Distribution

It is an erect shrub which grows to a height to 2 meters and has spreading or down curved leaves about 5mm long and 2.5mm wide. Pink or purple-red flowers about 15mm across are produced in rounded heads on the ends of the branches between August and December.

Kunzea recurva is a widespread but locally common, species, often found in wet depressions or on rocky slopes in the South Western, region of Western Australia. It ranges from Perth; south to Albany and southeast to Ravensthorpe. It grows in a variety of soil types.

It is not well known in cultivation.

Taxonomy and naming

Kunzea recurva was first formally described by the botanist Johannes Conrad Schauer and published in 1844 in Johann Georg Christian Lehmann's work *Plantae Preissianae*.

It is one of the species with the widest distribution and it shows considerable variations.

Hybrids:

A) Kunzea clavata x K. recurva – inflorescence, pale pink/yellowish pink with broad/flat leaves.

B) Kunzea ericifolia subsp. ericifolia x K. recurva. Leaves are varied - folded leaves resemble K. ericifolia; broad leaves, pink flowers and long hairs on floral bracts relate to K. recurva. **(Image Top P 161)**

C) Kunzea glabrescens x K.recurva – Leaves are flat, linear-elliptic & recurved; leaf bracts /bracteoles resemble those of K.glabrescens Pink/mauve flowers with hairy bracts/bracteoles are derived from K. recurva.

D) Kunzea micrantha subsp. oligandra x K. recurva – vigorous plants with broad & rigid branches and long hairs on the floral axis. Pink flowers. **(P 160)**

E) Kunzea micromera x K. recurva – robust, spreading habit with larger leaves & glabrous stems.

F) Kunzea montana x K. recurva – rigid & robust habit, absence of recurved margins on calyx lobes, but strongly recurved leaves with narrow, inconspicuous bracts. Pink inflorescences. **(Image bottom P. 137)**

G) Kunzea recurva x K. sulphurea - very common Tall shrubs, occurring in drier areas with K.recurva. Absence of recurved margins of the calyx lobes and the pale pink inflorescences. distinguish it from K. sulphurea. **(Images bottom P. 161)**

Kunzea micrantha subsp. oligandra x K. recurva

Kunzea ×*rosea* (Turcz.) Govaerts

Description & Distribution

Upright shrub to 1.3 m high and 2 m wide with black stems and many pink flowers in September & October., growing in heath with Hakea prostrata in plain grey sand. Found north-east of Albany and south of Ongerup and Jerramungup.

Cultivation

To the best of my knowledge Kunzea x rosea is unknown in cultivation

Kunzea rostrata Toelken

Description, Taxonomy & naming and Distribution & habitat.

This robust shrub grows to about a height of 3 metres. It flowers between October and November producing pink flowers.

Leaves: petiole to 0.5 mm long, appressed; lamina broadly elliptic to elliptic-obovate.

Inflorescence is spherical; flowers, terminal on usually lateral long shoots.
Calyx lobes; triangular to lanceolate, to about 3mm long, pointed to rostrate, ridged and usually with a subapical point, with incurved membranous margins and glabrous. Corolla lobes usually depressed obovate, and also about 3 mm long, Stamens number about 25-35 in more than one whorl.

Fruit an urceolate capsule with erect calyx lobes.

The species was first formally described by Hellmut R. Toelken in 1996 in the article *A revision of the genus Kunzea (Myrtaceae)* in the *Journal of the Adelaide Botanic Gardens*.

Often found growing in grey sands or peaty soils south-east of Busselton, generally between Cape Naturaliste and Cape Leeuwin.

Authors Note: I have included an image of a dried & mounted specimen of the plant seen in the West Australian Herbarium.

Kunzea salina (Trudgen & Keighery) de Lange & Toelken

Description, Taxonomy & naming, Distribution & habitat and Conservation

Low shrub to less than 1 m high, single stemmed base, with small, white flowers in November and December.

It was previously classified in the genus *Angasomyrtus* as *Angasomyrtus salina*. The name is still accepted by some authorities, while others accept its transfer into genus *Kunzea* as *Kunzea salina*.

Kunzea salina is located north of Esperance, growing in wetter areas of heath with low shrub land. The largest plants growing in the same location consist of species of Melaleuca, Hakea and Banksia.

K. salina is classified as "Priority Three" by the Western Australian Government Department of Parks and Wildlife, meaning that it is known from only a few locations, although not under imminent threat.

Photo's: Courtesy Mary Hoggart

Kunzea similis Toelken

Description, Taxonomy and naming; Distribution & habitat and Conservation.

Kunzea similis grows to a height of about 3 metres .Pink flowers between September and November...

The species was first formally described by Hellmut R. Toelken in 1996 in the article '*A revision of the genus Kunzea (Myrtaceae)*' in the *Journal of the Adelaide Botanic Gardens*.

K. similis grows in fine, clayey sand or grey loamy sand over laterite, on low slopes or ridge tops in the Ravensthorpe area south-east of Perth.

Photo: J Cochrane & G Cockerton. (P. 169 top left)

There are two subspecies. Both are considered rare as they are limited to single populations:

Kunzea similis subsp. *mediterranea* Toelken & G.F.Craig

A woody shrub, to 3 m high, with several stiffly erect main stems; moderately to few branched, with pink flowers from September to October - basal, lateral branches are usually without flowers. Young branches are densely covered with silky hairs. Flowers are pink.

K. similis subsp. mediterranea is confined to one population on Bandalup Hill east of Ravensthorpe.

Authors Note: *I was unable to access this location because it is now the site of a Bauxite Mine and is closed to the general public.*

Images: D Brassington, R Jasper & S Kern. (P. 169 top right)

- *Kunzea similis* subsp. *similis* Toelken

A woody shrub, to 1.5 m high, differing from K. similis subsp. mediterranea by its smaller bracteoles. There is a single population only, growing on heath on the lower slopes of East Mt Barren in Fitzgerald River National Park, in sandy-clay soil. Pink flowers October – November?

Authors Notes: *I travelled through Eastern side of Fitzgerald River National Park looking for Kunzea similis in October 2018 - over 60km; including about 40km of corrugated, car shuddering, body shaking gravel road. It was among the worst examples of gravel road I've ever driven on, and to make matters worse, I did not locate any flowering examples of this plant!*

However, the photo at the bottom of the opposite page was obtained at Kings Park in Perth.

*At the time, there was no signage found around the plants to assist with my identification, but from my observation there appear to be some similarities with K similis so I've placed the image here; however I have to refer to it as **Kunzea sp.** until properly identified.*

Kunzea spathulata Toelken

Description & Distribution

The shrub typically grows to a height of 4.5 metres. It blooms between October and November producing yellow to yellow-green flowers.

Often found around marshes and swampy areas in coastal areas of the South West corner of Western Australia – near the Towns of Augusta, Nannup and Pemberton.

Taxonomy and naming

The species was first formally described by Hellmut R. Toelken in 1996 in the article '*A revision of the genus Kunzea (Myrtaceae)*' in the *Journal of the Adelaide Botanic Gardens*.

Kunzea ericifolia var. glabrior is the only synonym.

Kunzea strigosa Toelken & G.F.Craig

Description, Distribution & habitat, Naming and Conservation Status

Kunzea strigosa can grow to a height of 1.3 metres with a few erect stems. It is very similar to *K. affinis* but distinguished from it by a hairy hypanthium and calyx lobes.
Leaves of K.strigosa are generally club-shaped. Flowering branches, rarely have more than one inflorescence on lateral branches, and flowers which are usually quite sessile. The flowers resemble those of *K. cincinnata* Toelken, but in the latter, the hairs are more or less coiled. The bracts and bracteoles are longer and pointed. Flowering period is August to November

I photographed K.strigosa in the Ravensthorpe area between Ravensthorpe and Hopetoun - east of the Fitzgerald River National Park. It has also been recorded west of Ravensthorpe near

Jerrumungup. It generally grows in sandy soil to clay loams on mid and lower slopes of ridges.

Naming: The specific epithet, strigose (means 'sharp, appressed hairs' in Latin). The fine hairs on the inflorescences are more rigid than the fine hairs on the leaves.

Conservation status: relatively widespread in the region and therefore not considered threatened.

Authors note: *Hopetoun and the Eastern side of Fitzgerald River National Park were the last places I planned to visit during this particular field trip. Unfortunately, it was here I experienced one of the most upsetting incidents of the trip. My accommodation did not have a Restaurant, so it was necessary to travel into the Town to have a meal at the local Hotel. However, one day a week the Hotel is; for whatever reason; closed, and visitors are required to travel to a small 'Bar & Bistro' about 3km out of Town. The day the "Pub" was closed I headed off to this alternative location – about 7pm. Suddenly there was this thump against the Drivers side of the car. I was stunned to see a big Kangaroo sliding along the side of the car. It had come out of nowhere. It must have decided to cross the road straight out of the 'bush'. Both the poor creature and myself were simply in the wrong place at the wrong time. I don't know what happened to the animal. All I can say is that it wasn't lying on the road. I stopped the car immediately to examine the damage, but couldn't see much in the dark. Fortunately the car was still driveable – all electronics etc. were working. I couldn't assess the panel damage to the vehicle until the following morning – I estimated about $5000 or $6000 though!*

Kunzea sulphurea Tovey & P.Morris
Description
Shrubs or small trees, about 2m to 4m tall, with few stems stiffly erect and with thin and
wiry lateral branches, much branched; young branches with decurrent flanges slightly
raised, usually densely covered with very short erect hairs; early bark fibrous-mosaic becoming thinly corky, very shallowly fluted.
Leaves: petiole, about 0.2mm to 0.5 mm long, appressed; lamina oblanceolate, rarely elliptic-oblanceolate, about 3mm x1.5 mm x 2.5mm, bluntly acute to rounded, gradually constricted into petiole and usually flat above. Inflorescence is spherical, with 12 to 23 flowers – mainly terminal – on lateral branches and usually not clustered.
Distribution

Growing usually in sandy soil in swampy areas or along streams often associated with forested areas from near Pemberton in a belt along the coast to near Mt Barker and Porongurup (excluding the area between Denmark and Albany) It blooms between September and November producing yellow flowers.
Diagnostic features

This distinct species has commonly been ignored and specimens identified as either K montana, K recurva or even K ericifolia. K. sulphurea is superficially similar to Kunzea montana but may be distinguished by its very short erect hairs on the branches, smaller flowers and more delicate bracts. The much less robust plant but yet a tall shrub or tree as compared with K. montana is easily distinguished from K. recurva by its broad rounded bracts and bracteoles and yellow flowers. The oblanceolate leaves and rounded bracts and bracteoles distinguish it from K. ericifolia. The specific epithet is somewhat misleading as flowers are pale yellow and have never been recorded as sulphur yellow.

Regelia

Regelia velutina

Regelia ciliata

Regelia ciliata Schauer

Description

Regelia ciliata is rigid, spreading shrub which grows to a height of 1.3–1.5 m. The leaves are arranged in alternating pairs so that they make four rows along the stems. They are broadly egg-shaped, about 6 mm long and 4 mm wide and fringed with short hairs.

The flowers are mauve and arranged in dense heads 20–50 mm across on the ends of branches which continue to grow after flowering. There are 5 sepals, 5 petals and 5 bundles of stamens. Flowering occurs over an extended period in spring and summer and is followed by fruit which are woody capsules in small, almost spherical clusters around the stem.

Taxonomy and naming

Regelia ciliata was the first of its genus to be formally described. The description was written in 1843 by J.C.Schauer in the journal *Linnaea: Ein Journal für die Botanik in ihrem ganzen Umfange*. The specific epithet (*ciliata*) is derived from the Latin word *cilium* meaning "eyelash" in reference to the fringe of hairs on the leaves.

Distribution and habitat

This Regelia occurs as far north of Perth as Geraldton in the Northern Swan Coastal Plain It grows in sand in areas that are wet in winter.

Use in horticulture

Regelia ciliata is a hardy plant, especially compared to others in the genus and has been grown successfully in eastern Australia. It can be propagated from seed which is released from the fruit a few days after removal from the plant, or from cuttings taken in autumn. It will grow in full sun or partial shade and responds well to annual pruning and addition of fertiliser.

Regelia cymbifolia (Diels) C.A.Gardner

Description

Regelia cymbifolia is much branched shrub which grows to a height of 2 m. The leaves are arranged in alternating pairs so that they make four rows along the stems. They are egg-shaped, usually less than 4 mm long, curved with their lower half pressed against the stem and have a prominent mid-vein.

The flowers are deep pink to purple and arranged in small clusters on the ends of branches which continue to grow after flowering. There are 5 sepals, 5 petals and 5 bundles of stamens. Flowering occurs between August and November and is followed by fruit which are woody capsules.

Taxonomy and naming

Regelia cymbifolia was first formally described in 1905 by Ludwig Diels in Botanische Jahrbucher fur Systematik, Pflanzengeschichte und Pflanzengeographie and tentatively given the name *Beaufortia cymbifolia*. In 1964, Charles Gardner recognised the specimen as *Regelia cymbifolia* in Journal of the Royal Society of Western Australia. The specific epithet (*cymbifolia*) is from the Latin words *cymba* meaning "cup" and *folia* meaning "leaf"

Distribution and habitat

Regelia cymbifolia occurs in a restricted area near the Stirling Range and in the Esperance Plains

It grows in sand on undulating plains.

Conservation

Regelia cymbifolia is classified as "Priority Four" by the Western Australian Government Department of Parks and Wildlife meaning that it is rare and endangered.

Use in horticulture

Regelia cymbifolia is not well known in cultivation but has been grown in Kings Park

Regelia inops (Schauer) Schauer

Description

Regelia inops is an upright, often spreading shrub which grows to a height of 0.75–2.5 m. The leaves are arranged in alternating pairs so that they make four rows along the stems. They are egg-shaped or triangular, and 1–4 mm long with their lower part pressed against the stem.

The flowers are mauve and arranged in small heads on the ends of branches which continue to grow after flowering and sometimes also on small side branches. There are 5 sepals, 5 petals and 5 bundles of stamens. The stamens, which give the flowers their colour, are about 6.5 mm (0.3 in) long and are joined for about half their length. Flowering occurs in the warmer months and is followed by fruit which are woody capsules, often in small, almost spherical clusters around the stem.

Taxonomy and naming

Regelia inops was first formally described in 1848 by J.C.Schauer in the journal *Plantae Preissianae*. He had previously given it the name *Beaufortia inops*. The specific epithet (*inops*) is a Latin word meaning "poor", "helpless" or "weak".

Distribution and habitat

This Regelia is widely distributed between Eneabba and Jurien Bay North of Perth. It grows in sandy soils on sandplains and in areas that are wet in winter.

Use in horticulture

The neat foliage and well displayed flowers make *Regelia inops* a suitable plant for gardens. It is easily propagated from seed or from cuttings.

Regelia megacephala C.A.Gardner

Description

Regelia megacephala is an erect, straggly shrub which grows to a height of 2–5 m.

The leaves are small and are arranged in alternating pairs so that they make four rows along its long stems.

The flowers are mauve and arranged in dense heads 15 mm across on the ends of long stems which continue to grow after flowering. There are 5 sepals, 5 petals and 5 bundles of stamens. Flowering occurs from September to December and is followed by fruit which are woody capsules.

Taxonomy and naming

Regelia megacephala was first formally described in 1964 by the Australian botanist, Charles Gardner in *Journal of the Royal Society of Western Australia*. The specific epithet ("megacephala") is from the Greek *(mégas)* meaning "large" and *(kephalḗ)* meaning "head".

Distribution and habitat

Regelia megacephala grows in red sand on rocky quartzite hills north of Moora – north of Perth.

Conservation

Regelia megacephala is classified as "Priority Four" by the Western Australian Government Department of Parks and Wildlife meaning that is rare and endangered.

Use in horticulture

Regelia megacephala is not often seen in cultivation but is frost hardy, will grow in full or partial sun and is suitable for narrow gardens. Its commercial potential for export as a Christmas flower has been assessed.

I have included an image of a dried and mounted specimen of R.megacephala from the Western Australian Herbarium.

185

Regelia velutina (Turcz.) C.A.Gardner Barrens Regelia

Description

Regelia velutina is a large shrub, sometimes a small tree, occasionally growing to a height of 6 m, with long, straight stems. Its leaves, are up to 13 mm long are arranged in alternating pairs so that they make four rows along the stems. The flowers are reddish-orange, sometimes yellow, and arranged in almost spherical heads on the ends of branches which continue to grow after flowering. There are 5 sepals, 5 petals and 5 bundles of stamens in each flower. Flowering occurs from September to November, sometimes to February and is followed by fruit which are woody capsules.

Taxonomy and naming

The species was first formally described by Russian botanist, Nikolai Turczaninow in 1852 who named it *Beaufortia velutina* In 1964, the Australian botanist Charles Gardner transferred it to the genus *Regelia*. The specific epithet (*velutina*) is a Latin word meaning "velvety".

Distribution and habitat

Regelia velutina grows in sandy soil in rocky areas, eastern side of Fitzgerald River National Park, near Hopetoun, SE of Perth.

Use in horticulture

Although it has attractive foliage and flowers, *R. velutina* is not common in cultivation. It does not grow well in areas of high summer rainfall and humidity. In drier climates it prefers well drained soils. It is easy to propagate from seed but the leaves may rot if mist propagation systems are used. Its commercial potential for export as a Christmas flower has been assessed.

www.ingramcontent.com/pod-product-compliance
Ingram Content Group UK Ltd.
Pitfield, Milton Keynes, MK11 3LW, UK
UKRC031939180426
11947UKWH00005B/20